Justification by Faith—
A Matter of
Death and Life

Justification by Faith—
A Matter of
Death and Life

GERHARD O. FORDE

FORTRESS PRESS   PHILADELPHIA

Second printing 1983

Library of Congress Cataloging in Publication Data

Forde, Gerhard O.
　Justification by faith.

　Includes bibliographical references.
　1. Justification.　2. Faith.　3. Grace.
4. Augsburg Confession.　I. Title.
BT764.2.F67　　1982　　234′.7　　81–70663
ISBN 0–8006–1634–0 (pbk.)　　AACR2

449C83　Printed in the United States of America　1–1634

CONTENTS

PREFACE

The litany of complaint against the doctrine of justification by faith seems once again to be on the increase. Objection to the doctrine, of course, is not new. Ever since Paul proposed justification as an interpretation of the cross and resurrection of Christ, it has been under fire. That is almost to be expected, since by its very nature the doctrine has a polemical edge.

Complaint today, however, seems to have taken a more subtle turn. Rather than being frontal and direct, the attack is now oblique. It can be summed up in the general charge that, even if true, the doctrine is biblically, temporally, and systematically too parochial and narrow. It is biblically parochial, runs the argument, because it is only one of many biblical images for the saving event. It is temporally parochial because it deals with problems of a bygone era—the consciousness of sin and guilt—and thus is not "relevant" to the modern age. It is systematically parochial because of the tendency to reduce theology to one issue.

This book is written in the conviction that the current litany of complaint places the church once again at something of a crossroads with respect to justification by faith. Either we must become more radical and serious about the doctrine or forget it altogether. To me the first option is the only viable one.

To be sure, the litany of complaint is not without some validity. The doctrine of justification has indeed been tied to modes of thinking and systematic structures that are too parochial. Perhaps justification has always been a proposal seeking an appropriate and satisfying structure. The basic thesis of this book is that the doctrine can be both radicalized and found more satisfying and universal in structure if it is complemented by the biblical and Reformation understanding of death and life. To be justified *is* a matter of death and life. The purpose of this book is to explore what that might mean for the thinking and preaching of the church.

In substance the book contains the Knubel-Miller-Greever Lectures for 1980, delivered on the occasion of the 450th anniversary of the Augsburg Confession. I am grateful to the Lutheran Church in America for inviting me to give these lectures both at my own institution and at sister seminaries in Waterloo, Canada; Columbus, Ohio; and Philadelphia, Pennsylvania. The hospitality and consideration shown me at each of these places was most gratifying.

This printed version of the lectures retains something of the flavor of oral delivery, though considerable material has been added here beyond what could be included in the spoken text. Readers who may be puzzled by the approach in the early part of the book, or be wondering about the "relevance" of it all, may find it helpful to read the last chapter first.

GERHARD O. FORDE
Luther-Northwestern
Theological Seminaries

1

MORALITY AND MORTALITY

Karl Barth in his epoch-making Commentary on Romans likened the institutional "remains" left by the event of revelation to the burned-out cinders left by a great explosion. The ecclesiastical practices and structures, the laws, dogmas, doctrines, and confessional documents are like the charred clinkers in a crater marking the fact that here a great explosion took place or a meteor crashed marking the divine eruption into time. Without necessarily espousing the implied view of revelation, I would suggest that Barth's image is a useful one. All too often, in interpreting the documents of the faith one can become so preoccupied with an examination of the crater and the cinders that one forgets the explosion. One scrambles about with archeological tools wondering what in the world actually happened here and what the fuss was all about. One attempts, perhaps, to construct an "objective" and dispassionate account of the earth-shaking event. The temptation is all the greater at those special times when we recall the landmark events of the Reformation.

If today, for example, we are to appropriate the witness of a document such as the Augsburg Confession in anything more than perfunctory fashion we cannot just investigate the crater. We must try somehow to recapture the explosion. Examining the crater and the cinders is a useful, indeed an absolutely indispensable exercise. There is no substitute for careful, linguistic, exegetical, and historical work. But we have to get beyond the research as such and put it to work in trying to grasp the explosion itself, recapture it so that it can be set off again and again in the life of the church. What once shook everything to the roots can do so again today.

Indeed, the constant temptation of the church seems to be to dampen the explosion, attempt to bring it under control, make it "safe" according to our timorous and cautious estimate of things. To use an image from atomic physics, we are always putting the rods into the reactor to bring it under control and render it useful for our own particular ends. When the explosion that gave us the Reformation has been so dampened and brought under control, it is not strange to find ourselves hundreds of years later wondering if perhaps it wasn't just a minor affair after all, localized in time and space, parochial in its application, or perhaps even something of a "dud." We find ourselves wondering about the "relevance," as we like to put it, of "old clinkers" such as the Augsburg Confession. When I ask graduating seniors at my seminary if they espouse the church's Confessions, I am apt to get some such answer: "Well, yes. I don't have any problems with them!" No problems! But where is the fire, the passion? It is like asking a husband, "Do you love your wife?" and getting the answer: "Well, yes. I don't have any problems with her!"

But how are we to recapture the explosion? Several ways might be attempted. Careful and minute historical investigation of the confessional documents and their context can do a great deal. But such a road is open primarily to experts. Imaginative reinterpretation and translation into modern idiom might achieve the purpose, but only if the work is well done. My intent in these chapters, however, is to try something different. I am not going to attempt yet another detailed exegesis of the *Confessio Augustana* (hereafter cited as CA) although I draw upon such works. Nor will I attempt just another imaginative reinterpretation, although I hope my project is indeed imaginative and a reinterpretation that has its own integrity. What is offered here is a bit more risky, at least from a scholarly point of view, because I wish to interpret the CA not so much in the light of what it says, as in the light of things it leaves unsaid— some basic aspects of Reformation theology which do not come to expression in it but are presupposed in the background.

My contention is that in the CA at least half of the Reformation story is missing. One of the vital ingredients that makes the Christian "powder" so explosive has been left out or forgotten. I am referring to the fact that the advent of the Christian gospel means, in addition to or along with justification by faith alone, also death and new life in the crucified and risen Christ—as suggested in the very title of this book. There are two basic metaphors (they are something more than metaphors but we will skip that for the moment) at the root of Pauline/Reformation theology. One we can call the moral or legal metaphor, which speaks in terms of law, morality, justice, and justification. The other is the death-life metaphor, which speaks in terms of mortality, dying to the old and rising to the new life in Christ and the Spirit. Reformation theology is generally formulated in terms of the legal metaphor, while the death-life language is left largely out of the picture. I am not particularly interested here in attempting to fix the blame for this omission. I am content to leave that to historical investigation. Perhaps in the case of the CA it was due to the polemical context, the relative dogmatic utility of the legal language for confessional purposes, or even to some confessor's (Melanchthon's?) preferences and/or the "relevance" of such language for the penitential ethos of the time. Perhaps the theologians of the period just took the death-life language for granted. The fact is that the legal language tends to become dominant if not exclusive in the confessional documents of the Reformation while the death-life language recedes and often disappears altogether.

My basic thesis is that the explosive character of the Reformation's confessional message can come to light once again if the death-life language is recovered and restored to its proper place. When such language and the reality it represents is revived and made complementary to the legal language, the theological explosion can take place once again. Certainly one can't make much sense of the CA without doing just that. These chapters will be an attempt to demonstrate this fact in at least a preliminary way.

The legal metaphor cannot stand alone. Where that happens, the explosiveness of the kerygmatic content is dampened and preachers tend to wilt and go on the defensive, capitulating before the attacks of the moralists; they lose, so to speak, their fire-power. The "relevance" of justification, when the message is couched only in legal terms, is soon lost.

3

Yet the death-life language cannot stand alone either, or we are left wondering what in the world it is supposed to mean. Standing alone, it generally tends to be frittered away in various kinds of mysticisms or asceticisms in which Christian spirituality is seen as the art of coming as close to self-destruction as possible without actually committing suicide! Left by itself, it too tends to become moralized: Death of the old comes to mean "mortification" of the "flesh," and new life is taken to be the reward of "mystical vision" accorded only to the accomplished.

When justification language is brought together with death-life language, however, so that justification by faith alone *is* death and resurrection, then one has a potent theological explosive. Our purpose in what follows will be to demonstrate this and to explore what it can mean.

The effort may also be a contribution to the problem of appropriating the confessional witness today, especially that of the CA, and with that, to say something about what we like to call its "relevance" (a horrible, usually misunderstood and misused word). There is good reason for such an attempt when one looks both at the history of the appropriation of the CA and at the contemporary context. From the very beginning it has been sensed that something was missing in the Confession itself. This sense has created an instability, an interpretational tug-of-war, so to speak, with attempts being made to pull the Confession this way or that according to the needs of the moment or the view of the particular interpreter. (Even the author himself, Melanchthon, tried to make changes later to reflect his own concerns in somewhat different contexts; indeed, his own Apology for the CA is much more forceful than the CA itself.)

The suspicion that something may be missing, something left unsaid, goes all the way back to Luther himself and his celebrated assertion that Melanchthon was a *Leisetreter*, one who was able to "tread more lightly" than Luther himself would ever have been able to do. What did Luther mean? Was his remark intended as a compliment or a complaint? The argument continues,[1] with no apparent solution. Lutheran interpreters tend to take the "treading lightly" reference as a complaint, a criticism, maintaining that the

Confession is too irenic and makes too many concessions for ecumenical purposes, glossing over thorny issues like the papacy, purgatory, and the sacrifice of the mass. Thus Heinrich Bornkamm maintained that the CA ". . . alone cannot be regarded as a sufficient presentation of Reformation teaching." At the very least, he says, ". . . one must take in addition Melanchthon's Apology, which is in many instances more forceful, his 'Treatise on the Power and the Primacy of the Pope,' and Luther's 'Smalcald Articles.' "[2] Bornkamm seems to think that what is missing is polemical bite and completeness. Melanchthon, for the sake of ecumenical rapprochement, left us with something of a toothless wonder!

Lutherans in North America have surely had their troubles with the CA.[3] Rarely have they been able to let it stand alone. At one extreme, I suppose, is the position of the Lutheran Church—Missouri Synod overtly insisting that the CA cannot stand alone and that the rest of the *Book of Concord* must be added as the key to correct interpretation and a fuller account of Lutheran doctrine. At the other extreme is the "American Lutheran" party of S. S. Schmucker which held that the CA should be improved by making a more modern and American recension. In between are various positions trying to maintain the integrity of the Confession but opting for more or less interpretational flexibility, more or less emphasis on additional confessional documents in the *Book of Concord*.

One can detect among Lutherans a kind of three-way tug-of-war over what is missing. One force would pull it back in the direction of the more polemical, anti-Roman stance of early Lutheranism. The second would like to pull it forward in the direction of the doctrinal completeness and "purity" of the later developments in the Formula of Concord. Yet another would pull it in the direction of modernization, interpretational "flexibility," and "relevance." All of that history raises the question of the contemporary appropriation of the confessional witness. What shall we do with the CA today?

Now, as if the historical difficulties Lutherans have had were not enough, ecumenical dialogue and rapprochement raises many of the old questions in a new and even more acute way. Recent discussion about possible Roman Catholic recognition of the CA reveals this clearly. The problem in essence is that (with some exceptions, of course—Article VII, for instance!) Roman Catholics tend to like just those things in the CA which make many Lutherans suspicious. The CA is, of course, an ecumenical document, and that is part of its great value. For many Catholics this has been, by and large, a pleasant new discovery. Catholic understanding of the Reformation has, through the years, been nurtured for the most part by catalogues of so-called heretical statements extracted from the more polemical writings of Luther, and Melanchthon dating from the early 1520s. To this day Catholics continue to be sensitive to and uneasy about what they still call these "exaggerated polemical assertions" (about, for instance, the bondage of the will and divine necessity, divine monergism, rejection of episcopal office, *sola fide*, and antinomianism. The CA was largely ignored outside the circle of a few specialists. When it is "rediscovered" today it appears to Catholics, of course, as a much more sane, irenic, and moderate "catholic" document—at least in most of the doctrinal articles. The very suggestion that Catholics should consider recognizing the CA is itself an historic event of great ecumenical moment, even if it has yet to meet with universal approval.

But the question of Catholic recognition creates further problems because it adds yet another dimension to the interpretational battle, yet another pull in the tug-of-war. Vinzenz Pfnür, the Catholic historian, who has written what is certainly one of the more valuable recent studies of the Augsburg Confession,[4] develops the thesis that the CA should be seen as a *corrective* over against those early "polemical exaggerations" of the 1520s. It will come as something of a surprise to Lutherans, no doubt, to be told that the CA is not just a "soft-pedalling" of early Reformation bombast, but actually a correction of it. The question of Catholic recognition consequently becomes a more complex issue for Lutherans. There is a certain pressure, sometimes subtle, sometimes not so subtle, *on Lutherans* from the Catholic side to recognize the CA as the correction of Lutheran excesses. Joseph Cardinal Ratzinger has rather explicitly suggested, in effect, that before there can be a Catholic recognition of the CA there ought to be a Lutheran recognition![5]

What Roman Catholics would like to hear from Lutherans, he says, is an interpretation of the CA in accordance with the ancient dogma of the church and basic church structure. Do Lutherans, he asks, have a normative doctrine? Concretely, what is the weight or rank of the CA as over against other confessional writings, particularly the Smalcald Articles written by Luther himself? Since Catholics tend to view the CA as a corrective to early excesses, they want assurance that in cases of conflict or dispute Lutherans will not revert to Luther rather than to the CA. The result is a tendency to drive a wedge between Luther and the CA which is disconcerting. Even some Catholics sense this and raise objections. Peter Manns, for instance, pointedly asks whether the intent of the movement toward Catholic recognition of the CA under such auspices is not simply to create an *oikumene* at the expense of Martin Luther.[6] Luther always seems to be the "odd man out."

So in addition to the interpretational tug-of-war among Lutherans there is also the pull in the direction of a more "catholic inter-pretation, the "correction" of early Reformation excesses. This tug in the direction of a more "catholic" interpretation as a proposed corrective to the "exaggerations" of early Lutheranism is particu-larly awkward just at this time, of course, since within theology itself the rediscovery of early Lutheranism, particularly the theology of the young Luther, the theology of the cross, and the hermeneu-tics upon which it is based, has played a major role in the shaping of contemporary Protestant thought. Precisely this *early* Lutheran theology has been an important source and a powerful influence assisting Protestants to overcome stagnation and rigidity on the one hand and loss of substance in "liberal" reductionism on the other. Ironically, the very theology that has helped to keep Luther-anism in the "catholic" fold is the theology which Roman Catholics seem desirous to pull Lutherans away from. But that can only mean that what hangs in the balance is just what the CA *tried* to bring to expression—the root concern of the Reformation movement. It is fair to say that this *particular* tug-of-war in which the CA is being pulled either in the direction of early Lutheranism or in that of more conservative and authoritarian Catholicism is one of the more important battles today. A CA recognized by the Roman

Catholics and interpreted by the authoritative teaching office of the Church, subsequently to be filed discreetly away in the back of its doctrinal handbooks and histories, is of little use to the church or the ecumenical movement. Indeed such a recognition could be one of the most effective ways possible to dampen the Confession's explosive potential.[7] It would become just another clinker.

So, in the midst of this confusing tug-of-war over the CA, it is important to get our bearings and ask ourselves about the appropriation and transmission of the confessional witness today. How do we go about that? On which rope in this at least four-way tug-of-war are we going to pull—in the direction of early Lutheran polemics, late Lutheranism, modernization, or a more "catholic" or ecumenical interpretation? It seems to me that what we need today is somehow to transcend these battles without losing what is essential and life-giving for the church and the *oikumene*. As Ratzinger suggests, past history cannot be ultimately determinative in the interpretational tug-of-war. There is always the possibility on the basis of the Reformation heritage to break new ground which might leave some of the old battles behind while at the same time preserving what is vital to the church and permanent in that heritage.[8] It may even be that the real vitality and reforming fire for the church is precisely in those "polemical exaggerations," and that what is needed is a view that can recover the real point of such assertions.

An understanding of the complementary nature of justification and death-life language might furnish the answer. To be sure, it is not an easy answer for either Catholics or Protestants. We might all begin to realize that even for the ecumenical life of the church it is a matter of death and life—that what it will really take for us to come together at last is to die to the old and to be made new. But we have nothing to fear from that, for *the* death has already been died for us; what remains is only to live.

There is risk in talking not about what the Confession does say, but what it seems to have left unsaid. By taking that risk, however, we may be able to transcend the tug-of-war at least to some extent. If it is the "something missing" that has provided the occasion for the interpretational tug-of-war, perhaps one can best attack the problem by dealing more directly with that "something missing" and thus assist in at least relaxing some of the tension. To pick up again on Barth's image, what is missing is one of the vital ingredients of the explosion. If we could somehow recapture that ingredient or get a little glimpse of it at least, it might give us pause in our argument about the cinders.

Now where does the problem lie in all this? The root problem is always the same—the one that was evident from the beginning: it is the *sola fide*, the claim that we are justified, as the CA says, ". . . freely for Christ's sake through Faith . . ." (Art. IV). The problem is the *sola fide*, the faith *alone*. It is precisely that *alone*, that *sola*, especially when combined with *faith*, that makes us think there surely must be something missing and leads us, both Protestant and Catholic, to rush in with all our interpretative additions. Surely one can't seriously mean *alone?* Particularly *faith* alone? Roman Catholics, of course, insisted from the outset that the *sola* was not enough. Faith, they insisted, must be "formed by love"; it must produce good works, and such good works must in some sense be meritorious. Something must be *added*.

What is the difficulty? The difficulty, to a large extent, is that the language, the legal metaphor, tends to fail us just at the crucial moment. We set the whole matter up as a legal process, the process of becoming "just" according to the law, making progress, doing good, and then at the last moment we suddenly turn and say it is impossible by that route to become just and that one is instead justified *by faith alone—sola—*and the *sola* means apart from works, love, or merit. One sets up the scheme and then destroys it by saying we get it all by faith anyway. Small wonder that people down through the ages have gotten nervous, and in subtle ways tended to hedge on the *sola* and thus dampen the explosion. The basic problem is that when we think in terms of the legal metaphor, as we all inevitably do, justification by faith never seems to be enough. And this, it must be said, is as true for Protestants as it is for Catholics. "But, don't we have to *do* something?"—the question always bubbles to the surface out of deep moral and self-protective undercurrents. And in the face of the question we usually "chicken out" little by little and lose the battle for want of explosives. Even when we attempt to stick with *faith alone* we are usually driven to define, qualify, and hedge about the faith of which we speak so that no one will get the "wrong idea." Of course we don't mean just any old faith, we mean *really* believing; we mean a really sincere, heartfelt trust, we mean a living, active faith, a faith which comes after deep and despairing repentance—all that "adverbial" theology. Before we are through we have so qualified and modified faith as to make it even less obtainable than the justice we failed to reach by the law! No wonder most people today would rather take their chances with the law! Faith itself has been taken captive by legalism. The price is so inflated that no one can afford it any more. In the face of the qualifications of such faith, the onslaughts of legalism and moralism, the explosion is dampened, tamed, and lost. Protestants eager to attest their orthodoxy and "safeness" are drawn into the same game, put on the defensive, and the battle is lost. Maybe not "faith formed by love" but "really sincere faith" at least!

The point is that justification *sola fide* cannot be understood or its explosive power captured in terms of the legal metaphor alone. One always seems to have to back down from that exclusive *sola*. For what does *sola fide* mean when you come right down to it? It means precisely not some sort of legal transaction but, according to the New Testament, a death and a resurrection. *Sola fide* pushes you to that critical point. What did Paul do when he was confronted by the questions that buzz about like angry flies whenever the legitimacy of such faith is at stake? He didn't backtrack and hedge and qualify it to death. He sailed right ahead and raised the questions himself (Romans 5). He even framed them in more audacious terms than his opponents might have done: "Shall we continue in sin that grace may abound?" (Rom. 6:1). That is about the most radical form in which the question could be put—the last question one could raise! Not just that we *might* get lazy and lax if we get too much grace, but shall we "*continue* in sin" in order to get all that much more grace!

And what is the answer? It is certainly not that faith must be formed by love, or completed by works, or that you must become more sincere, *really* sincere, or *really* repent, or that there is after all the law or the "third use of the law," so you had better mind your p's and q's just in case. No, the answer comes in terms of death and resurrection:

> Are we to continue in sin that grace may abound? By no means! How can we who died to sin still live in it? Do you not know that all of us who have been baptized into Christ Jesus were baptized into his death? We were buried therefore with him by baptism into death, so that as Christ was raised from the dead by the glory of the Father, we too might walk in newness of life.
>
> For if we have been united with him in a death like his, we shall certainly be united with him in a resurrection like his. We know that our old self was crucified with him so that the sinful body might be destroyed, and we might no longer be enslaved to sin. For he who has died is freed from sin. But if we have died with Christ, we believe that we shall also live with him. For we know that Christ being raised from the dead will never die again; death no longer has dominion over him. The death he died he died to sin, once for all, but the life he lives he lives to God. So you also must consider yourselves dead to sin and alive to God in Christ Jesus. (Rom. 6:1-11).

When the question is put whether grace and faith is perhaps too dangerous or too cheap, or whether people might take it for granted or trade on it, Paul answers in terms of death and resurrection: "How can you who *have died* to sin still live in it?" Paul does this repeatedly. He doesn't argue the case. He doesn't lay on more law, insisting that we *ought* to die to sin or the law, or to "mortify" the flesh. He simply announces that we already have died: "The love of Christ controls us because we are convinced that one has died for all; therefore all *have died*" (2 Cor. 5:14). In other words, just at the crucial point, the point where justification by faith has destroyed the whole legal scheme and we are getting terribly nervous and beginning to back down, dampen the explosive message, put rods in the reactor, Paul steams ahead and shifts almost imperceptibly to death-resurrection language without even breaking stride. He does the same thing in Gal. 2:16 ff:

> We have believed in Christ Jesus, in order to be justified by faith in Christ, and not by works of the law, because by works of the law shall no one be justified. But if, in our endeavor to be justified

11

in Christ, we ourselves were found to be sinners, is Christ then an agent of sin? [That is, does grace lead to laxity?] Certainly not! But if I build up again those things which I tore down, then I prove myself a transgressor. [That is, if I now "chicken out" on grace and justification by faith, then I am really a transgressor. If I succumb to the law and legalism I *really* sin! But what then is the answer? Paul steams right ahead:] For I through the law died to the law, that I might live to God. I have been crucified with Christ; it is no longer I who live, but Christ who lives in me; and the life I now live in the flesh I live by faith in the Son of God, who loved me and gave himself for me. I do not nullify the grace of God [that is, I absolutely *cannot* do that!]; for if justification were through the law, then Christ died to no purpose.

The death-life language takes over where the legal language is broken and begins to falter. Where we reach the end of the legalistic rope and are searching nervously and desperately for some way to continue our self-appointed program, there we come up against the reality of being crucified and raised with Christ. "For Christ is the end of the law—to those who have faith" (Rom. 10:4). But *only* Christ—the one who died under the law and rose—is the *end* of it!

Here we come upon that certain something which is more or less left unsaid in the CA, which can help us to transcend a lot of the argument among interpreters—that tug-of-war we talked about —if we recover it and interpret the CA in its light. For if you look around in Reformation theology, especially early Lutheran theology, you will see that it too, like Paul's theology, is basically stamped by this death-life language. Indeed one could argue that this language is the real root from which Protestant theology grew in the young Luther's theology of the cross. But it is not necessary to push that point here. It is sufficient to maintain that this death-life language is *one* of the roots of Lutheran theology which we often don't know what to do with. We leave it out of the picture by default, or tend to submerge it under the legal metaphor altogether.

To see just how basic such death-life language is to Reformation theology one need look no further than the understanding of the distinction between law and gospel as that grows out of Luther's early struggles with interpreting the scriptures—what we now like to call the development of his hermeneutics. The search for the proper distinction between law and gospel is, in essence, nothing other than a search for an understanding and use of theological language that gives life beyond the death always administered by legal talk or law. It is a search for a use of language in church discourse, in proclamation, which does not merely talk about life or describe life but actually gives it.

One can see this quite clearly by looking at the way in which the law-gospel distinction developed out of the old dichotomy between letter and spirit in the tradition.[9] Paul's passage in 2 Cor. 3:6: "The letter [written code, law] kills, but the spirit gives life," was the starting point and the storm center around which the dispute raged through the years. It is to be noted that the passage *is* about death and life, about killing done by the letter or written code and life given by the spirit. However, under the legal metaphor one doesn't know what to make of death. Indeed, the *point* of the legal or moral way, the way of the law, is to *escape* death, to earn the justice that deserves an "eternal" reward. Now, of course, one can't make much progress or earn many points if one "ups and dies," or if by the letter, the law, the written code one is "killed" rather than given new opportunities. You see, under the legal metaphor, and the understanding of life it brings, it is the *law* that grants possibility, not the gospel, and that possibility is necessarily curtailed if someone dies! The order for the legal metaphor is always life-death. You can do the law only as long as you are alive; you have to earn your points while you can. For the legal metaphor is a matter, as we say, of "life and death." When you die it's too late. If you die you shall not live. The law grants possibility up to death; after death, no more possibility.

Consequently, the Pauline passage about the letter killing and the spirit giving life had to be understood some other way. One had to find a way to apply it to people who don't really die. So instead of taking the passage at face value, as designating the *action* of the word (killing and making alive), it was taken to designate different levels of *meaning* in the word—the literal meaning and the spiritual meaning, in accordance with the Platonic dualism between the material and spiritual that dominated ancient thought. Thus the scriptures came to be interpreted as having different levels of meaning, a purely outward material, or literal meaning and a spiritual, heavenly, or inward and "life-giving" meaning. The task of interpretation was to search for the appropriate method to get from one level to the other. That the letter kills was taken to mean that the mere literal or historical meaning was dead or inadequate. One must learn how to get from the mere "dead" letter to the true, inner, eternal, and spiritual meaning.

Thus a way was found to apply the words in such a way as to avoid death. That is to say, a way was found to make the scriptures "relevant" to the Old Adam—a dubious and mistaken enterprise which has continued in various ways to the present time. The word is taken to be a surface phenomenon, a secret code, enlightening the spark of the Divine in us—a gnostic procedure which, in spite of our rejection of Gnosticism, continues often to be the basic hermeneutic down to our own day!

Following Origen much of the tradition interpreted the antithesis between letter and spirit in a Platonizing sense: The letter "kills" because it is limited to the sensible world. If one remains stuck with it alone one will perish in the land of appearances. One must somehow pass beyond the sphere of what is perceptible to the senses and get over to the intelligible world, the world of eternal truth, eternal ideas, where the finite spirit cavorts with "eternal spirit" and there is no death. (No one seemed to notice that there was no life either!) The method of interpretation, it is to be noted, was also a covert soteriology—almost always that turns out to be the case. The idea was to escape death by penetrating to the level of life-giving spirit via interpretation, hermeneutics. The attempt was to do this by allegorical exegesis. The mere literal, especially where it was offensive or obscure, was by allegory, tropology, and anagogy to be raised to the level of the spiritually life-giving. This means that the historically unique was for the most part insufficient, or at best only a sign or surface manifestation of an eternal truth, doctrine, or law. To be rendered salvific the "accidental truths of history" had to be translated into "eternal truths of reason," to use Lessing's later distinction. It was a means to escape death.

Now to make a long story extremely short and perhaps somewhat oversimple, Luther in his own struggles, came to see through this whole scheme. One does not get "life-giving spirit" by interpretation. For if that is so, the system only turns out to be more law. The method of interpretation or the rules of exegesis or perhaps the mystical way of life implied in the interpretation then becomes the new law. Then only the clever, the educated, the ones who can exegete accurately will get the "life-giving spirit"—*if* they don't make any mistakes![10] The method of interpretation itself yields only more law, and instead of giving life it only brings more death. This is what Luther found in his struggles with the problem of interpretation. The "spiritual" and "moral" or "penitential" flight prescribed by the tradition was not only unscriptural but impossible and personally destructive.

Luther's own move was quite simple. He took the 2 Cor. 3:6 passage to mean just what it says: "The letter *kills,* but the spirit *gives life.*" What the passage describes is an *action*—not a more or less esoteric method of interpretation. The letter, the written code, kills and *through it* the spirit gives life. The letter is not something obscure or weak or insufficient. It is not *dead* because it belongs to the sensible world. Rather, it is *deadly,* it kills. If the letter has the power to kill, it can by no means be taken lightly, nor can it be circumvented or shunted aside by interpretation. The letter, the whole long history of God's struggle with his people culminating in the cross, spells in the first instance but one thing for the Old Adam. It spells death. The hermeneutic itself is shaped by the death-life language. It takes the shape of the cross: the letter kills the old, and through it, when one at last meets the end of one's sinful ways, the spirit, the life-giving word is given. The scriptures do not provide a mere "jumping-off place" for flights of allegorical and exegetical fancy; they rather cut off such flight. "Spirit" is not some secret inner "level of meaning" that one reaches by intellectual or mystical exercise. The Spirit is precisely the Holy Spirit of God, the Author of the scriptures who uses them as his two-edged sword. The Spirit comes in and through the letter, in and through the concrete history culminating in the cross and resurrection, in and through the proclamation of it to kill and make alive.

It is that fundamental understanding of the scriptures and use of the language which stands behind the Reformation. It is not just a matter of certain formulas, not even *sola fide!* It can readily be seen that the very use of language itself is shaped by the metaphor of death and life, not by the legal metaphor. The distinction between law and gospel in proper communication of the word is simply a further application of this language. The fact that the letter kills but the Spirit gives life, Luther says explicitly, can be said in other words: The law kills, but the grace of God gives life.[11] The letter-spirit problem so vexing in the tradition issues in the law-gospel dialectic fundamental to preaching and communicating the word. Not just what the word *means* is important—and the sorting out of levels of meaning or fancying such levels—but what the word *does*. And what does it do? It kills and makes alive. That is what lies behind the law-gospel language, not merely the legal metaphor, but the theology of the cross.

One could run through many aspects and writings of the early Reformation period and show how this death-life language appears everywhere and in crucial places. Indeed we will do some of that in the following chapters. Here we would make just a couple quick references to pin down the point. In *The Babylonian Captivity of the Church*, speaking of Baptism, Luther says:

> Baptism thus signifies two things—death and resurrection, *that is, full and complete justification*. When the minister immerses the child in the water it signifies death, and when he draws it forth again it signifies life. Thus Paul expounds it in Rom. 6 [:4]: "We were buried therefore with Christ by baptism into death, so that as Christ was raised from the dead by the glory of the Father, we too might talk in newness of life." This death and resurrection we call the new creation, regeneration, and spiritual birth. *This should not be understood only allegorically as the death of sin and the life of grace*, as many understand it, *but as actual death and resurrection*. For baptism is not a false sign.[12]

Extremely significant in a passage like that are a couple of things. First of all, "full and complete justification" is equated with death and resurrection, not with a legal scheme as such. Secondly, and also of utmost importance, is the statement that this death and resurrection (new creation, regeneration, spiritual birth) is not to be understood as an allegory, but as an actuality. As we might put it, the death and resurrection is not just a "symbolic" one, it is not merely, as Luther puts it, a symbol for the death of sin and the life of grace, some "internal transformation," but it is itself the reality. The death and resurrection, that is, is more than a metaphor, a symbol, an allegory, for something else, some "profound transformation" of some sort or other, some "rebirth" which means only "giving in" at last to law and "conscience." It is the reality itself. Full and complete justification *is* death and resurrection. What Luther seems to be saying here is that death and resurrection is the primary reality and even takes precedence over the legal language. If death and resurrection were just an allegory or a symbol for the putting off of sin and the life of grace, then the legal scheme would be the reality, and the death and resurrection a symbol. But Luther will not have it so. Death and resurrection is the primary reality. Thus he says a bit later on: "It is therefore indeed correct to say that baptism is a washing away of sins, but the expression is too mild and too weak to bring out the full significance of baptism, which is rather a symbol of *death and resurrection.*"[13]

Death and resurrection posits a radically different understanding of the way of salvation. Under the legal metaphor, the subject is a continuously existing one who does not die but is merely *altered* by grace. Salvation, you might say, is something of a *repair* job. Quite naturally then, one will want to magnify that repair job and speak of the "transformation" in as glowing and positive terms as possible. To speak of justification *by faith alone* could then seem only as though one were reducing everything down to a kind of bare minimum, a sort of cut-rate salvation, a "cheap grace" to use the phrase popularized by Bonhoeffer. The mistake is to think that we can remedy the charge of "cheap grace" by making it expensive, by inflating the rhetoric, piling up the adverbs, reimposing the law, until the enterprise takes on the aspect of a great balloon which rises on the strength of its own hot air! Death and resurrection as a real event, however, proposes quite a different way. As those famous words from Luther's *Bondage of the Will* have it:

> When God quickens, He does so by killing; when He justifies, He does so by pronouncing guilty; when He carries up to heaven, He does so by bringing down to hell. As Scripture says, "The Lord killeth and maketh alive; He bringeth down to the grave and bringeth up" (1 Sam. 2:6). . . . When God kills, faith in life is exercised in death.[14]

17

The subject does not survive intact on its own steam, undergoing only certain "alterations." What is involved is rather a matter of death and life. There is new life. That the subject is made new is due to the action of God, the resurrection in Christ, not to repairs made according to the legal scheme.

This calls for a fundamentally different strategy in theologizing and preaching. One would not want to magnify and glorify the repair job or try to obviate the charge of cheapness by making grace expensive or inflating the rhetoric. One would rather be called upon to make talk about grace as radical, as unconditional, as free and pure as possible. If you are out to lay the old to rest and give new life, you will speak and act quite differently. That is what lies behind the *sola fide* and the CA. The gospel grants the ultimate possibility, not the law. It is not a matter of life and death but a matter of death and life. It is not that one must merely live to avoid dying, but that unless we die we shall not live. If we can recapture this, perhaps we can recapture some of the fire—and not back down.

Of course talk about death (particularly death) and new life is difficult for us to handle. We have a kind of aversion, a kind of blind spot, to such language. Maybe that is one reason for its relative absence even in the church. We tend not to see it when it stands right before our eyes. No doubt with good (or not so good!) reason. Who likes death? We fear it; we shy away from it. As Ernest Becker has so eloquently pointed out, most of our life's energy and cunning is spent in denying it.[15] We are like Howard Hughes, that pathetic modern parallel to the Rich Fool. We are so afraid of death and so caught up in defending ourselves against it, hiding from it, and denying it that in the end it kills us! Theologically speaking I expect we fear talk of death because in our rather incurable tendency to think only in terms of the legal and moral scheme we treat death as only a metaphor for one more legal, moral, or mystical process. As if it weren't bad enough to be told we have to fulfill the law, now we are told we have to die! How can we do that? So also we tend to look upon the theology of the cross as though it proposed just one more burden, one more impossible project, this time an excessively gloomy and morbid one at that! Perhaps one could say we shy away from the death so much that we never find what the new life is about.

So we get trapped in the legal language. The death-life language becomes strange and even forbidding, perhaps at best a weird form of mysticism. We can't seem to get from one to the other. Albert Schweitzer put the problem in that fashion long ago in his book on *The Mysticism of Paul the Apostle* and perhaps contributed much to "poisoning the wells." Paul, he maintained, held two independent and contradictory views of the new righteousness, one based on what we have called the legal metaphor (justification by faith) and the other based on a "mystical" dying and rising with Christ.[16] It is impossible, Schweitzer avers, to get from one to the other. The point of these lectures, however, is that we must do so, indeed, that the two must be taken together as complementary to one another if the explosive nature of the confessional witness is to be at all recaptured. Indeed, it is only when they are taken together that each really receives its due.

2

LIVING, WE DIE:
JUSTIFICATION BY FAITH ALONE

We have already mentioned the place and prominence of death-and-life language in the early Lutheran movement. It would be tempting to let such language displace the legal language altogether. Yet this clearly cannot be done—at least this side of the Parousia. Thus we must contend for and attempt to fix the place of the legal language as well, the language of justification by faith alone. Thus we have spoken of the complementarity of the two types of language as one way of dealing with the matter because when the question is put about just what this talk of death and life means one is hard pressed to answer this side of the Parousia without resorting to justification language. One must say curious things like "justification by faith alone," or speak of the manner in which the legal language under which we live reaches its absolute end and limit in faith. "Christ is the end of the law to those who have faith; I through the law died to the law that I might live to God"—such is the way one is driven to speak.

So in the present chapter we will look a little more closely at the question of justification and some of the problems involved in the legal language as it appears in the confessional statements. We can do no better than to begin with Article IV, the heart and core of the Augsburg Confession (quoting from the translation of the Latin version):

> Our churches also teach that men cannot be justified before God by their own strength, merits, or works but are freely justified for Christ's sake through faith when they believe that they are received into favor and that their sins are forgiven on account of Christ, who by his death made satisfaction for our sins. This faith God imputes for righteousness in his sight (Rom. 3:4).[1]

We are justified freely, for Christ's sake, by faith, without the exertion of our own strength, gaining of merit, or doing of works. To the age old question, "What shall I do to be saved?" the confessional answer is shocking: "Nothing! Just be still; shut up and listen for once in your life to what God the Almighty, creator and redeemer, is saying to his world and to you in the death and resurrection of his Son! Listen and believe!" When one sees that it is a matter of death and life one has to talk this way. The "nothing" must sound, risky and shocking as it is. For it is, as we shall see, precisely the death knell of the old being. The faith by which one is justified is not an active verb of which the Old Adam or Eve is the subject, it is a state-of-being verb. Faith is the state of being grasped by the unconditional claim and promise of the God who calls into being that which is from that which is not. Faith means now having to deal with life in those terms. It is a death and resurrection.

The "nothing" is a radical, controversial, explosive, and even disconcerting answer. It has always been so. We should make no mistake about that. It was so when Paul first shocked the synagogues and temples of his time with it and got beaten and thrown out for his pains. It was so when Augustine provoked Pelagius (and later semi-Pelagian camp-followers of all sorts) into that pious and moralistic defense which in one way or another, with a subtlety ever more refined, repeatedly insinuates itself into the life and doctrine of the church like a creeping paralysis. It was so at the time of the Reformation, and—though rarely stated with vigor—it is so today. All one has to do to test the shock effect is to try talking about that "nothing" in its "purity" even in churches of the Reformation, or writing about it in official organs of the church! Once recently I was asked to talk about justification and predestination as one finds them in Reformation doctrine. The topic provoked rather hefty and heated argument. After my talk was over a nice old gentleman came shuffling up to me and said, "You know, I can't figure it out. Why is it that when anyone talks about the sheer grace and absolute mercy of God people get so mad?"

Why indeed? Because it is a radical doctrine. It strikes at the root, the radix, of what we believe to be our very reason for being.

The "nothing," the *sola fide,* dislodges everyone from the saddle, Jew and Greek, publican and pharisee, harlot and homemaker, sinner and righteous, liberal and orthodox, religious and non-religious, minimalist and maximalist, and shakes the whole human enterprise to the roots. It strikes at the very understanding of life which has become so ingrained in us, the understanding in terms of the legal metaphor, the law, merit and moral progress. Justification, the reformers said, is by imputation, freely given. It is an absolutely unconditional decree, a divine decision, indeed an *election,* a sentence handed down by the judge with whom all power resides. It is as the later "orthodox" teachers like to say, a "forensic" decree: a flat-out pronouncement of acquittal *for Jesus'* sake, who died and rose for us. As precisely that kind of unconditional decree it puts the axe to the root of the hegemony of legal language. Paradoxically, if not perversely, it seems to attack and destroy the very language on which it depends. It speaks about *justice,* about *justification,* seemingly to imply *becoming just* according to the law or some legal process, and then at the last moment shatters the whole thing by saying justification *by faith,* not by the works of the law! It seems to pit the justice of God and his decisions against the justice we poor struggling humans have tried to carve out for ourselves.

The unconditional language is what causes us so much trouble. This is precisely the point at which we are sorely tempted to put the damper on the explosion, put rods in the reactor. Whenever one speaks about such things—especially in the church—one can virtually predict the questions and the protests. "But . . . , but we have to do *something,* don't we?" "Are there not after all *some* conditions?" "Isn't *faith* or at least *sincere repentance* a condition?" Don't you at least have to "decide?" Don't you have to "make your decision for Jesus?" The difficulty is exactly with the unconditional nature of the decree: You are justified for Jesus' sake! As Robert Jenson puts it in a recent study on the Confessional writings, our lives in this age are shaped by *conditional* promises and statements.[2] Conditional promises are "if-then" promises. *If* you fulfill the required conditions *then* the promise will be fulfilled. "*If* you eat your spinach . . . , *then* you will get your dessert." *If* you put the coin in the slot, *then* you will get the candy bar. *If* you study hard, *then* you will get good grades and maybe a scholarship to Yale or Harvard. *If* you do your job well, *then* you will get a promotion or a raise, or get called to a big city congregation or be made a bishop or a full professor. Always 'if-then." Almost everything we live with is conditional and so it must be here.

The gospel of justification by faith is such a shocker, such an explosion, because it is an absolutely *unconditional* promise. It is not an "if-then" kind of statement, but a "because-therefore" pronouncement: Because Jesus died and rose, your sins are forgiven and you are righteous in the sight of God! It bursts in upon our little world all shut up and barricaded behind our accustomed conditional thinking as some strange comet from goodness knows where, something we can't really seem to wrap our minds around, the logic of which appears closed to us. How can it be entirely unconditional? Isn't it terribly dangerous? How can anyone say flat-out, "You are righteous for Jesus' sake? Is there not *some* price to be paid, *some*-thing (however miniscule) to be done? After all, there *can't* be such a thing as a free lunch, can there?

You see, we really are sealed up in the prison of our conditional thinking. It is terribly difficult for us to get out, and even if someone batters down the door and shatters the bars, chances are we will stay in the prison anyway! We seem always to want to hold out for something somehow, that *little bit* of something, and we do it with a passion and an anxiety that betrays its true source—the Old Adam that just does not want to lose control.

When we deal with such things as justification and righteousness we are bound by our inevitable tendency to think in terms of the legal metaphor. We think of becoming righteous or just according to the law, according to some scheme or movement, movement up the ladder of the law or virtue or morality so that the higher one gets on the scale, the more righteousness, the more justice and virtue and morality, and consequently the less sin one has. On such a scale righteousness and sin are mutually exclusive. The more you have of one, the less you have of the other.

It is against just such thinking, however, that the statement found in CA IV is directed, as is the entire doctrine of the Reformation. If you take a good look at Melanchthon's Apology you will see that very clearly. The whole burden of his "Apology" for Article IV is that the opponents don't make the proper distinction between law and gospel and that they think exclusively according to the law, the legal metaphor. This was precisely the thinking with which Luther had such trouble, and the argument against it is the explosive that blows everything apart.

It is important to see this today precisely in the context of the ecumenical discussion. Many Roman Catholic interpreters like to say that it was the late medieval distortions and Pelagianizing of the legal scheme which caused all the trouble. It is true that those late medieval excesses provided the immediate occasion for the protest that triggered the Reformation, but it was not just the excesses that must take the brunt of the charge; it is the entire legal scheme itself. Even in its finest form, the scheme causes trouble. Thomas Aquinas, for instance, defines justification as a movement from a *terminus a quo* to a *terminus ad quem* (a movement from a starting point to a finishing point) involving several steps: a) the infusion of grace (grace *does* come first); b) movement of the free will toward God in faith; c) movement of the free will in recoil from sin; and d) remission of guilt.[3]

The problem is that in such schemes justification can be understood only as a movement. One can do everything possible to make sure all the movement is by what is called "grace;" one can say that grace gives the beginning, furnishes the power to continue, and realizes the end. One is justified "by grace, through faith." But the movement remains. One can even say, as Aquinas did, that the movement is not really a movement in time but that all the "steps" happen simultaneously, all at once and not in a series. Yet the fact remains that it can be understood only as that kind of movement, and the way is open, no doubt, for precisely those distortions which *did* occur in the late Middle Ages. For how can a movement not be temporal?

It is important to make this point precisely in the context of the ecumenical discussion not because we want to hold out for some sort of polemical anti-Catholicism, or flatter ourselves about the rightness of Reformation teaching, but exactly because the problem is just as prevalent (if not more so) among Protestants as it is among

Catholics. The defenses against which the explosive charge was hurled are as much in place now as they were then. If the CA is to have any significance for us at all today, this is precisely what must be seen. We cannot all sit around smilingly and say we agree with one another when it may be that we agree only because we have all missed the point! We *all* have the incurable tendency to think in legal fashion, in terms of movement. We all tend to think, as Luther put it, *ad modum Aristotelis* (in the fashion of Aristotle)[4] because we think that the degree of sinfulness or righteousness we attain depends on movement up and down a scale of virtue. Everything depends on what we *do* according to such a scale. Righteousness is real only to the degree that sin is expelled. Now the Christian, of course, would want to add, no doubt, that movement up the scale is "by grace," perhaps even "by grace *alone*," but it is, nevertheless, the movement that is the reality. The legal metaphor holds sway to the end.

Now it is impossible to combine this thinking in terms of movement according to the legal scheme with justification by divine imputation, by an unconditional decree or election. The legal thinking causes problems both existentially and systematically. Existentially the problem comes if I am honest enough to realize and confess that the scheme just doesn't seem to work as well in actual life as it does in our theological books. I am promised progress and improvement "by the power of grace" but what if I actually don't seem to be getting anywhere in particular? Talk about grace becomes just the problem! I keep trying, perhaps, and I go to church to get this thing called "grace" but it just doesn't seem to work. What then? The church assures me that there is nothing wrong with the "delivery system." The "grace" is there, especially in the sacraments. Not even a bad priest—say one who has committed mortal sin—can frustrate the delivery. That being the case, I could come to one of two conclusions, or perhaps a mixture of both. One, and perhaps the most plausible, is that the fault must lie with me. Perhaps I just have not done the proper things, or done enough to get this thing the theologians call "grace." Perhaps I just don't know the right "combination." But suppose I do as much as anyone else, or more. Suppose I really do everything prescribed, and even more, and I still don't seem to make any progress. What then? Then I might come to the second possible conclusion, the one much more terrifying: Perhaps the reason lies with God! Perhaps God, the giver of all such grace—at least so I am told—has decided not to give it. Perhaps God has turned thumbs down. Once one thinks in terms of the "process," grace *alone* is no comfort because then I must progress while someone else provides the power—which is like trying to drive the car while someone else's foot is on the accelerator. The more one exalts grace *alone*, the worse it gets.

You see, when the attempt is made to combine justifying grace with the legal scheme or idea of "movement," grace turns to poison; it deserts me when I need it most. In the final analysis, *everything* will depend either on me *or* on God. I am left suspended between a futile quest for self-salvation or the terrors of predestination. One simply cannot successfully combine a grace freely given with the legal scheme. As Paul put it, "If justification were through the law, then Christ died to no purpose" (Gal. 2:21b).

To use a rather far-fetched illustration, it would be something like saying that you have to grow freckles in order to be saved. Well, then, if you don't have them (by some mysterious predestination) the question would be, "How do I get freckles?" 'By grace," comes the answer. "But where do I get such grace?" "From God." "But how?" Well, you go to church and partake of the sacraments and pay attention to the preacher and do what he says." So I do all that and the next morning I look in the mirror and behold, no freckles! Now what? Then there are just the two possibilities. Either I have not followed the instructions properly, or God has just decided not to give this mysterious freckle-creating grace to me. I am left between the devil and the deep-blue sea: my own failure and the terrors of predestination. Usually, of course, I will be pious and gracious enough to flatter God by not laying the blame on him and grit my teeth in resignation and take the blame on myself. So in the end everything will depend on me.

The point of the illustration is that when one attempts to combine freely given grace with an empirical legal scheme (the demand to grow freckles) *everything* will come to depend on me in the end, no matter how much one *talks* about grace. When one

27

thinks that way, even the freely given grace becomes poison, it turns into a terrifying thing. God, I am told, gives his grace freely to everyone. God loves everybody. There is nothing wrong with the delivery system either. "All systems are go!" But *I* don't get freckles. What am I to conclude? It makes no difference then how much one exalts grace or what you can say about it. You can say that grace makes the beginning, grace is free, grace makes the progress, and grace puts the finishing touches on those strange spots. But every such statement about grace, given that system, is just another nail in the coffin. Statements about grace only remove me from it all the more. Either that or I will begin to suspect the truth: there *is* no such thing; the "grace" so talked about is a fiction—or at least a terribly inadequate and misleading way of describing what it is that God does for us. The problem is in the language, the metaphor, the very idea that something other than faith is required—that faith itself is the point—not freckles, not the law—that the *you* God created is good, good enough, and the problem is precisely the failure to believe it. The problem is the incurable religiosity itself. Its all beside the point—the you God created is good. Can we actually believe it? Can we believe in God the Creator?

Systematically, the problem is similar. It is impossible to combine justification by faith with the idea of movement according to the legal scheme. For if we have to do with a movement, the question—simply put—is, where does justification come? At the beginning or the end of the movement? If, on the other hand, justification comes at the beginning of the movement it would seem that no movement is necessary—the movement itself is superfluous. If I get it all at the beginning, why move? If, on the other hand, justification comes at the *end* of the movement, then it would seem that justification is superfluous. Why do I need to be justified if I have already arrived at the end of the movement anyway? You don't need to be *declared* just if you already *are* so. The fact is that justification and movement cannot *both* be real. One simply renders the other superfluous. Of course there have been and still are attempts to work out compromises of one sort or another, but the history of such attempts is not encouraging. Generally law tends to remain the dominating reality and grace dwindles off into the status of a pious fiction. After all, we have to do *something*, don't we?

Now we do not get the radicality of the confessional point in Article IV unless we begin to grasp the fact that what lies behind it is a complete break with all thinking in terms of the legal scheme and the idea of movement and progress that goes with it, a break with all thinking *ad modum Aristotelis*. Thus Luther, when he was struggling with both the existential and the systematic aspects of the problem came to the conclusion that all the schemes of movement from sin to righteousness, all thinking exclusively in terms of that legal or moral metaphor, had to be abandoned if grace and justification are to have any reality at all. In the place of all such schemes, in the place of the conditional thinking that always traps us, we must put the absolute *simultaneity* of sin and righteousness. When God acts upon us with his grace, with his justifying deed, his pronouncement, we become *simul iustus et peccator*, simultaneously righteous and sinner. What is revealed ultimately to faith is, paradoxically, our incredible and persistent lack of faith. When the word of promise comes or begins to dawn on us, our reaction is "I can't believe it! You mean that's all?" As when the word of a lover, "I love you!" comes to one who is always trying to become more lovable, and the response is: "I can't believe it—it's too good to be true." The word of promise engenders faith and at the same time reveals to faith the truth of the situation—the power and persistence of sin (unbelief). It reveals the duality. Grace is not a mysterious supernatural power which operates somehow secretly behind the scenes. Grace is the divine pronouncement itself, the morning star, the flash of lightning exploding in our darkness which reveals all truth *simultaneously*, the truth about God and the truth about us. Since righteousness comes just by divine pronouncement, by divine "imputation" as Luther liked to put it, it cannot come either at the beginning or end of any of our schemes of "movement." It establishes an entirely new situation. It can be received *only* by faith, suddenly "seeing" the truth. It is not a movement on our part, either with or without what was previously called "grace." It is a re-creative act of God, something he does

29

precisely by speaking unconditionally. It is like the "let there be light" which reveals the darkness to be darkness simultaneously with its own lightening.

It is of great importance to see that the *simul iustus et peccator* is not a conclusion drawn from our failures under the legal system as a kind of sop to the "anxious conscience." That, I am afraid, is the way it is often treated. Leaving the legal scheme intact we come to realize at least now and then that we can't really do *everything* —after all, nobody's perfect!—so we settle for saying, "Oh well, we are *simul iustus et peccator!* Isn't that what Luther said after all?" Taken that way it is a counsel of despair, cheap comfort for lazy sinners. It boils down to the platitude that there is some good in the worst of us and some bad in the best of us. But that means only that the *simul* is used as a rescue for the legal scheme instead of a complete departure from that scheme.

The *simul iustus et peccator* is not a conclusion drawn from failure under the law, but rather a confession flowing precisely from the unconditional nature of the divine promise, the divine act of justification. Thus, already in the Romans Commentary where Luther first propounded the *simul* he suggests that what is required by the divine action is a different kind of thinking. Instead of thinking *ad modum Aristotelis* he proposes a thinking *ad modum scripturae* (in the fashion of the scriptures). In the scriptures the divine imputation (cf. Rom. 4: 1–7) is the creative reality which by the very fact of the imputation unmasks the reality and totality of sin *at the same time*. For Luther the deduction of the *simul* follows quite logically and has nothing particularly to do with the much celebrated "anxious conscience." Since God has to *impute* righteousness we must be sinners. It would make no sense for him to impute righteousness if we were already wholly or partially righteous or even had some hope of becoming so according to our legal schemes. It would make no sense for God to forgive sins if we weren't actually sinners. He would simply be wasting his breath. Thus exactly in order that God "may be justified in his words" and "true when he judges" the thinking *ad modum Aristotelis* must be jettisoned when we come to the question of justification. One must somehow learn to think *ad modum scripturae*. Before the divine tribunal no saints, but only sinners can stand!

30

Justification by unconditional decree means a complete break with thinking in terms of the legal schemes and processes. The most vital enemy of the grace of God, Luther insists throughout his commentary, is not so much the so-called godless sinner, but precisely the "righteous" who think in terms of a legal process, an "intrinsic" moral progress which renders grace fictional and gradually unnecessary. "For if justification is by the law, Christ died to no avail (Gal. 2:21)." When the divine judge speaks his unconditional word, all the world must simply be silent and listen![5]

If we can begin to wrap our minds around that perhaps we can be grasped by the radicality, the audaciousness, the explosiveness of the confessional point. When God imputes righteousness he makes us sinners at the same time. He makes it quite plain that we do not have righteousness in ourselves and never will. By declaring us righteous unilaterally, unconditionally for Christ's sake, he at the same time unmasks sin and unfaith. By forgiving sin, sin is revealed and attacked at the root in its *totality:* our unfaith, rebellion, and blindness, our unwillingness to move out of the legal prison, our refusal of life. God's justification, you see, is fully as opposed to human righteousness and pretense as it is to human unrighteousness. It cuts both ways, both at the ungodly and the super-godly. The battle is not against sin merely as "moral" fault but against sin as "spiritual" fault, against our supposed "intrinsic righteousness," pretense and hypocrisy, our supposed movement and progress, our substitution of fiction for truth. The totality of the justifying act reveals the totality of sin. Imputed righteousness makes it plain that all such "piety" is just as sinful, indeed even more sinful, than out-and-out godlessness and denial of grace altogether. Only faith in the flat-out judgment of God is equipped to do battle with human sin. One can only be still and listen to the judge. That is the only salvation from both despair and presumption, immorality and super-morality. In the light of the creative, unconditional divine act it becomes clear not just that we have sinned and fallen short of the law, but precisely that "all have sinned and fallen short of the glory [precisely the *glory*] of God" and all he has created. By speaking unconditionally, the Creator is doing again a new thing.

It should be clear from this that in the light of the divine action we can be saved only by listening to him, only by faith in his word of acquittal, his word of justification. There is no other way. Perhaps we can make this even plainer by recalling the discussion in Romans 7 where Paul talks about the law and how one fares under the law. The law says "Thou shalt not covet." Now what effect does that have on one who is a sinner? Paul says that he would not have known sin had not the law come to prohibit covetousness. As a matter of fact, the law only served to work "all manner of covetousness" in him. In other words, the sinner, under the law, only becomes worse. How are we to understand that? It is a mistake to take it only in a psychologizing fashion, that is, that the law only arouses the sin it prohibits (forbidden fruit is always sweeter). That may indeed be the case in some, most, or even all instances. But Paul is not concerned to make only that obvious point. He is not so naive as to say that before the law about covetousness came he had no lust for this or that, no sin. Rather what he is saying is that the law provides absolutely no help, no way out for sinners. Because even if I, as a sinner, try to obey the command "Thou shalt not covet" and earnestly and zealously pursue the goal, I do not escape because now I only covet a certain goal, a certain image, a certain perfection for myself. Now, you might say, I covet being a noncoveting person. I covet "sainthood." So I have not escaped at all. Sin is only aroused all the more, and precisely the law, even though it is good, arouses in me "*all* manner of covetousness." So even though I recognize that the law is good, I see—if I am honest—that I am "carnal," sold in sin. I can agree with the law, and can even will the good, but I can't *do* it, because under the law, the very commandment that promises life brings death. Since I *am* a covetous person, the command "Thou shalt not covet" can at best only change the object of my covetousness. But in the end there is little difference *coram deo* whether I covet my neighbor's wife or my own righteousness. Indeed, the latter may be the most dangerous of all since it is the most praised among hypocrites. Now then, the point is that the law simply cannot save sinners. The only way is simply to listen to the judge and believe him when he speaks. As Paul concludes: "Wretched man that I am, who shall deliver me . . . ? Thanks be to God it is through Jesus Christ our Lord!" The unconditional word of justification is the *only* way.

It is, I suppose, the very explosiveness and radicality of this unconditional act that causes us all the difficulty. Perhaps it is precisely because we are so totally exposed for what we are! At any rate it seems to be just at the point where we begin to glimpse the radicality of it all that all the questions and protests begin to spew out: "We have to do *something*, don't we?" Stuck in our old ways of thinking *ad modum Aristotelis* justification by faith can only appear terribly dangerous and even threatening. Is the justifying word *absolutely* unconditional? Aren't there some little conditions after all? Is not imputed righteousness "cheap grace?" What about morality? What about good works? Virtue? The building program? Won't people (usually called the "simple folk" or "the ordinary layperson") get the wrong idea?

It is in the face of such questions that we are tempted to "chicken out" and go on the defensive and thus lose the battle little bit by little bit. When the question comes, "But . . . , but, we have to do *something*, don't we?" we are most likely to say, "Well, yes, now that you mention it, there *is* a little something. You have to bake cookies for the bazaar, bring your pledge up to date, and maybe go to church at least once a month." And then we are through. We may as well quit, for then and there the battle is lost.

The point, the confessional point, is to stick with it and sail into the storm with all guns blazing. "We have to do something, don't we?" NO! In fact that is no longer the question. Now the question becomes, "What *are* you going to do now that you don't *have* to do anything?" Theology based on the CA is not interested in "something"; it is after *everything*. A pastor friend related an interesting reaction from a teenager to *Free to Be,* a little book on Luther's Catechism by James Nestingen and myself. He said he didn't like the book because it seemed to tell him he could do anything he wanted to do! Now what is one supposed to say to that? The most immediate reaction, I suppose, would be to jump in on the defensive and thunder, "No! No! No!—of course not, you can't do whatever you want to do!" But think for a moment. Perhaps then the whole battle would be lost. One must sail into the storm. Should one not rather say "Son, you are right. You got the message. The Holy Spirit is starting to get to you." For now, you see, the question is: "What *do* you want to do? Who *are* you now that God has spoken his word to you?" But is that not dangerous? Of course it is! But God has taken a great risk to get what he wants. We can only follow him in that. Is it not "cheap grace"? No! It's not cheap, it's *free!* "Cheap grace," you see, is not improved by making it expensive, a "bargain basement" special. It's *free*. Now free grace *is* dangerous, no doubt about it. To follow out our image, it is an explosion, and such explosions are dangerous. We might not survive such free grace. It might ruin us. But Jesus told us that long ago: "To him who has, more will be given, but from him who has not, even that which he has will be taken away." There is indeed a danger. We worry constantly about morality and good works. But Paul has already put the question: "Shall we continue in sin that grace may abound?" And that is the right question. It is the only question left to ask. And the answer? No, by no means! Why not? Because how can we who died to sin still live in it?

So we arrive at that point again. The answer to all the impetuous questions is not at all a defensive one. It is the one last step, the final attack: You have died! We arrive again at the point we reached in chapter 1. When the legal language, the legal metaphor reaches its end, the death-life language emerges quite naturally to take over. This is the final explosion, the final (literally!) *coup de grâce* (stroke of grace). As we said already, however, we don't usually know what to do with this death language. Usually we try to translate it back into the language of law or morality, or perhaps mysticism, and we speak of mortification of the "lusts of the flesh" or mystical steps of purgation—as though only "part" of us has to go, our vices but not our virtues. Now it is precisely here that the complementarity of the unconditional declaration of justification and the death-life language must be grasped. For the point is that the unconditional declaration of justification, the imputation, the flat-out declaration, that which offends and shocks us so, that which shatters all our ambitions for "something to do"

—that declaration *is* our death and our life, the new beginning. It is the act which re-creates, redeems God's creation. Death, you see, is put in the position of not being able to do anything according to the ways of this world—the law, religion, the upward climb—with all its plans and schemes. They suddenly stop, come to an end: "I through the law died to the law that I might live to God." Both our vices and our virtues come to a full stop. The justification declaration *is* precisely that: a full stop. "You have died," says Paul. It is all over!

Thus the contradiction posited by Schweitzer between justification language and death-life language can be overcome—but only when it is seen that the declaration of justification *is* death and resurrection. The *simul iustus et peccator* is really also *simul mortuus et vivus* (simultaneously dead and alive). "So you also must consider yourselves dead to sin and alive to God in Christ Jesus" (Rom. 6:11). The justifying pronouncement and the death-life are complementary and not contradictory. The declaration of justification, the sheer unconditional imputation by "the word alone" cuts off the endless extension of the legal metaphor at the same time as it prevents the death-life language from lapsing into a new mysticism or a new legalism of even more strenuous proportions (some purgation of the "lusts of the flesh," some negative theology of glory such as taking the task of "dying" on oneself). One does not now have to die in some mystical fashion or another; one is already dead to the old in and through the justifying pronouncement— simply by believing it. Unconditional justification puts the old absolutely to death. It is the only death (the major death) we will live to tell about!

At the same time, the reality of such death and new life prevents the imputed and forensic justification from being appropriated as "cheap grace" by the Old Being. Since it is a matter of death and life, there is no cheap grace for the Old Adam or the Old Eve. "How can you who have died to sin still live in it?" Grace is not made "expensive" by sneaking in a bit of law to shore up the sagging enterprise. The absolutely *free* character of the justifying word administers death to the old and gives life to the new.

The old argument about whether justification is "only" forensic or also "effective" is thereby transcended. When one sees that justification and death-life are complementary it is then apparent that the absolutely forensic character of justification renders it effective—justification actually kills and makes alive. It is, to be sure, "not only" forensic, but that is the case only because the more forensic it is the more effective it is!

That the early Reformation looked upon justification this way can be amply documented, as we saw already in looking at Luther's statement about Baptism in *The Babylonian Captivity* (The "captivity," by the way, is precisely captivity to the scheme of law), and the development of the law-gospel distinction. Here we must look at one or two other prominent examples. Commenting on Gal. 2: 20, Luther says:

> "I am crucified with Christ." Paul adds this word because he wants to explain how the law is devoured by the law (Christ). If Christ is crucified to the law, so also am I. How? *Through faith.* I am crucified to the law; I have nothing to do with it, because I am crucified to it and vice versa, because I have died with Christ *through grace itself and faith (per ipsam gratiam et fidem).* . . . If you believe in Christ then you are co-crucified through faith spiritually, just as he is dead to the law, to death, . . .[6]

Receiving and believing the word of justification *is* death and resurrection. It is the end and new beginning. Nor is this spiritual death and resurrection to be confused with a kind of imitation or following of Christ's example in "mortification of the flesh." All of that is indeed to follow, but must not be confused with the death and resurrection administered by the justifying word itself. Luther says quite explicitly:

> Paul is not speaking here of the *imitatio*, which means to become co-crucified. That happens in the flesh, as Peter (1 Pet. 2:21) says: Christ suffered for you leaving you an example that you should follow in his steps. Here Paul does not speak of *that* crucifixion, but of the *primary* co-crucifixion by which the devil and death are crucified. Where? In Christ, not in me. That crucifixion by which I die to the law *is* resurrection, because Christ has killed my death and bound up my law. And I believe that.[7]

To hear and believe the word of justification for Jesus' sake *is* to die and be raised in him. Since he has died and been raised not even that can be turned into some kind of law, some "way" for us to traverse. It is not an *action* or movement on our part but simply a *passion*, a "suffering it to be so," a being slain and raised up. Faith arises out of that passivity. Faith comes by hearing! But at the same time it must not, as Luther said, be looked upon as being merely "allegorical" or "symbolic." The death inflicted by the justifying word which reduces us to nothing is the *real* death, the true *spiritual* death, the death of sin, the death of all defiance against the God who "will have mercy on whom he will have mercy." Since it is the death of sin, it is also the death of death. The other death, the physical death of the body that we must die at the end of our days, is for Luther a more minor matter. He called it *das Todlein*, the "little death." The *spiritual* death encountered in the unconditional address of the justifying word is the major death, the death we experience. Everything depends, for us, on whether we survive that word and believe.[8]

When we finally begin to grasp that justification by faith *is* death and resurrection we have an explosive mixture indeed, powerful enough to blast away once and for all the defenses which, in our timidity, we always tend to throw up against the unconditional justifying word. Here is where the battle for the confessional position is won or lost. Here is where the relevance of that position is decided. The persistent questions always put us on the defensive. But what are those questions, after all? When one looks at them from the perspective of death and resurrection one can begin to see that they are nothing more than the last gasp, the protesting death rattle of the Old Adam or Old Eve who knows the kingdom of the legal metaphor to be under radical attack. The Old Adam or Eve in us can't survive in the face of that attack and so clings desperately to the last hope. "We have to do *something*, don't we?" How like us, in the last extremity to bank on that little "something" we had planned to get away with! Our very questions expose us! The divine declaration does exactly what was claimed: it shows us to be *sinners* who have fallen short of the *glory* of God. We turn up a fantastic treasure in the field and we gawk at it like a cow staring at a new gate muttering, "Well, I suppose I have to do something, don't I?" We are bidden to the great feast and we have a thousand excuses. We are blind because we refuse to see.

So to return to the question of the old gentleman: Why does everyone get so mad? What we have to realize at last is that the experience of the unconditional word itself, the experience of being so absolutely frustrated, depotentiated, nonplussed, upset, yes, offended, by the address *is* exactly the point. It *is* the death knell of the old and the harbinger of the absolutely new, but somehow we have never quite realized that. Trembling on the brink of this freedom, we panic and turn back. Perhaps we are afraid that there *is* really something new, something quite other than we had planned. The summons comes, "Awake, thou that sleepest, and arise from the dead and Christ shall give you light!" Get out of your stinking tomb! But we mutter, "No, you see, I kinda like it here!" Perhaps what we tremble at most is resurrection! As on being awakened from a sound sleep, we would rather slumber on, oblivious to the glorious dawn. But the unconditional word, the promise, the declaration of justification is that which makes new, that which puts the old to rest and grants newness of life. Nothing matters now but that. As Paul put it, "neither circumcision nor uncircumcision," neither vice nor virtue matters at all, "but a new creation!" It is a matter of death and new life.

In the face of the questions that always beckon us to turn back and go on the defensive, it is necessary, therefore, to steam ahead. Perhaps here too the old word holds true: The best defense is a good offense! Don't give them the ball, for the stakes are great. Of course, such a position raises a lot of further questions, not the least, indeed, about what during the Reformation they called "good works," and such things as "growth" in the Christian life. Here too, perhaps more than anywhere else, there has been a tendency to falter and lose the way—precisely because we have not been grasped deeply enough by the fact that it is a matter of death and new life.

3

DYING, WE LIVE:
SANCTIFICATION AND GOOD WORKS

There is an old story about a Lutheran pastor who on his deathbed declared his confidence that he would go to heaven because he could not remember ever having done a good work in his life! The problem of sanctification and good works seems always to be the Achilles' heel of the Reformation and the Confessional doctrine. That's the point at which we are most likely to go astray, the point at which the most persistent attacks are directed against us and we become nervous, the point where we most often go on the defensive, make our fatal compromises, and lose the whole battle.

Here too we can recall the judgment of Albert Schweitzer who maintained that there was no road from redemption to ethics or good works as long as one remained with the legal metaphor, the language of justification by faith. "The doctrine of justification by faith, redemption, and ethics are like two roads, one of which leads up to one side of a chasm, and the other leads onwards from the opposite side—but there is no bridge by which to pass from one side to the other."[1]

So we need to look again at the Confessional teaching of the CA in Article VI on "The New Obedience" and Article XX on "Faith and Good Works." Once again, these articles can neither be understood nor upheld in the face of all the questions if one does not see them in terms of the complementarity of the legal and the death-life language. If one persists in thinking only in terms of the legal metaphor—*ad modum Aristotelis* as Luther put it—one cannot but make fatal compromises which reduce both grace and good works. One ends with a mixture of some sort: a certain percentage of grace and a certain percentage of "good works" in which *neither* gets full value and we end up crowding out one or the other altogether—most often the grace!—or maybe even losing both, as the contemporary world so painfully shows.

In more ways than one justification by faith alone is still a matter of death and life today. It is a matter of death and life for the church to recover the explosive doctrine, the unconditional grace that fosters true sanctification and good works, life beyond death. We begin our consideration of sanctification by looking at some of the Confessional statements.

> Article VI of the CA says concerning New Obedience: It is also taught among us that such faith (that is, faith created by the unconditional justifying promise—Article IV—communicated through the office of ministry—Article V—) should (Latin: is bound to) produce good fruits and good works and that we must do all such good works as God has commanded, but we should do them for God's sake and not place our trust in them as if thereby to merit favor before God. For we receive forgiveness of sin and righteousness through faith in Christ, as Christ himself says, "So you also, when you have done all that is commanded you, say, 'We are unworthy servants'" (Luke 17:10). The Fathers also teach thus, for Ambrose says, "It is ordained of God that whoever believes in Christ shall be saved, and he shall have forgiveness of sins, not through works but through faith alone, without merit."[2]

From Article XX on "Faith and Good Works" we select the following passages:

> Our teachers have been falsely accused of forbidding good works. Their writings on the Ten Commandments, and other writings as well, show that they have given good and profitable accounts and instructions concerning true Christian estates and works. About these little was taught in former times, when for the most part sermons were concerned with childish and useless works like rosaries, the cult of saints, monasticism, pilgrimages, appointed fasts, holy days, brotherhoods, and so forth.

> It is also taught among us that good works should and must be done (Latin: it is necessary to do good works), not that we are to rely on them to earn grace but that we may do God's will and glorify him. It is always faith alone that apprehends grace and forgiveness of sin. When through faith the Holy Spirit is given, the heart is moved to do good works. Before that, when it is without the

40

Holy Spirit, the heart is too weak. Moreover, it is in the power of the devil, who drives poor human beings into many sins.

Consequently this teaching concerning faith is not to be accused of forbidding good works but is rather to be praised for teaching that good works are to be done and for offering help as to how they may be done. For without faith and without Christ human nature and human strength are much too weak to do good works, call upon God, have patience in suffering, love one's neighbor, diligently engage in callings which are commanded, render obedience, avoid evil lusts, and so forth. Such great and genuine works cannot be done without the help of Christ, as he himself says in John 15:5, "Apart from me you can do nothing."[3]

The articles state the reformation position quite forthrightly and sometimes even courageously. Even so, one can hardly escape the impression that now and then they already betray a certain uneasiness and anxiety and tend to go too much on the defensive. They seem always to be groping for just the right language that will say neither too much nor too little, but they have a hard time finding the needed formula. "Faith," according to the German version in Article VI, "*should* produce good fruits and good works and . . . we *must* do all such good works as God has commanded." The Latin version says the same with a slightly different twist: "This faith *is bound* to bring forth good fruits and . . . it is necessary to do the good works commanded by God. We *must* do so because it is God's will. . . ." Article XX says: "Good works should and must be done . . . ," and having said that quickly adds that we are to do such good works for God's sake, not our own, and we are not to place our trust in them as if to merit favor before God. After such brief sorties into rather dangerous territory, the articles usually retreat to safer ground by reasserting the *sola fide*. (In this regard it is interesting to note that the *sola* appears explicitly together with *fide* in the article on good works, not in the article on justification!)

No doubt there is good reason for the anxiety, the uneasiness, the faltering attempts to arrive at a proper formulation. It is terribly difficult to break the hegemony of the legal terminology and the idea of moral progress. From the beginning, Roman Catholic suspicion has been focused on just this point. "How," Catholics persist in asking, "can one speak of justification by faith *alone*?" Does not faith have to be "formed, completed, shaped, by love?"

When confronted with that, as we all know, the reformers dug in their heels all the more and usually went even farther "to the right" in insisting on a justification that is absolutely forensic, a divine decree, pure and simple, without any conditions whatsoever, any mixture of human accomplishment. Touch that nerve and the characteristic Lutheran knee-jerk reaction is to move even farther in the direction of purely forensic justification. But that reaction, of course, only aggravates the question about good works and sanctification.

Here perhaps more than anywhere else the so-called exaggerated polemical overstatements of the early days continued to rankle. Speaking against the nominalist idea that one must "do what is in one" *(facere quod in se est)* in order to gain grace, Luther had flatly replied, "Whoever does what is in him commits mortal sin."[4] Now a good Catholic would no doubt agree that one can do nothing to earn the grace of God. But is it not an exaggeration to say that even to try is to commit mortal sin? On another occasion Luther says, "Faith and works are to the highest degree opposed. Therefore works cannot be taught without harming faith." Bugenhagen states: "There are two people between whom there will never be a unity, namely, faith and works." Melanchthon puts it this way: "All the works of humans, however praiseworthy they always are in appearance, are yet entirely sinful and worthy of death." Catholic polemicists have gathered catalogues of these kinds of statements from the early days of the Reformation.[5]

Then of course there is that shocking advice from Luther to Melanchthon that has always frightened tender souls: "Be a sinner and sin boldly, but believe even more boldly and rejoice in Christ who is victor over sin, death, and the world."[6] That sort of statement, too, has always seemed something of an exaggeration, perhaps for polemical purposes only.

In the debate with Erasmus, Luther had said things that could hardly endear him to the legal and moral mentality. When Erasmus asked who will be good, who will seek to reform self and do good if all those things about divine necessity and predestination are published, Luther shot back without flinching, "Nobody! Nobody can! God has no time for your practitioners of self-reformation, for they are hypocrites. The elect, who fear God, will be reformed by the Holy Spirit; the rest will perish unreformed."[7] That has seemed hardly to be a responsible answer! Perhaps at this point the reply to Schweitzer would be not only that there *is* no bridge of the usual sort between faith and works, but that the Reformers were bent on destroying whatever might have been left of such a bridge from the earlier tradition. That is just the point—for the bridge implies that the Old Adam is still alive to cross it!

Above all, the *simul iustus et peccator* brings with it an understanding of sin that undermines all ordinary ideas of progress according to moral or legal schemes. The *iustitia* exists *simultaneously* with the *peccatum*. The unconditional act of justification exposes; by declaring us to be just, it reveals us as sinners. In the light of the totality of justification, sin is confessed simultaneously as a total state. The justifying deed therefore does not remove sin in the sense one might accord a moral or legal scheme; it exposes it. As if the more light you get, the more dirt you see! And the miracle is that God nevertheless does business with sinners—in just that way!

When one thinks in terms of the legal scheme, however, one is inclined to say that grace is given to *remove* sin. The more grace you get, the less sin. There must be, as Roman Catholics like to say, a real progress, a real transformation.[8] If there is not, grace does not effect anything *real* at all.

So there is a remarkable stand-off here. For the reformers, the mark of being grasped by the grace of justification is precisely to be able to say at last, "I am a sinner, always have been, always will be, and can be saved by faith alone. And that is the real truth. That *is* reality." For the traditional Roman Catholic view, to be grasped by grace would have to mean that some real transformation is effected so that its mark would be to say, perhaps; "We are being transformed by the grace of God. If this is not true, there is no reality to it at all." Because of this stand-off it was quite understandable that the disputants at the time of the Reformation got into arguments about whether grace actually removed original sin, whether the concupiscence remaining after Baptism, for instance, was still sin or only the "seeds" or "tinder" of sin. Lutherans argued that it was sin, but that the guilt was removed. Catholics argued that then nothing *real* happens and that one must rather say that the *sin* is indeed gone even though the evil tendency, the tinder, the seeds, remain. The difficulty is that what the one view takes to be the mark of grace the other takes to be the mark of its absence. The crucial question, ecumenically, is whether this stand-off can be mediated at all. But the idea contained in the *simul*, that sin remains as a total state *simultaneously* with the justification by faith, of course raises the question of good works, progress, and sanctification. The old question comes back to haunt: "We have to do something, don't we?" Is there no such thing as progress in the Christian life?

Catholic suspicion and the constant fire of moralists have gradually taken their toll on the confessional position. All too often Protestants have not had the courage of their convictions. They have gone on the defensive, made concessions, and ended by adopting one form or another of the patronizing rhetoric of their adversaries, usually for the sake of so-called "practical" exigencies. It just isn't "practical" to preach or teach an "unconditional" promise. Confronted with the problem of moral laxity after the early days of the Reformation, Protestants, who didn't want to revert to saying that you have to earn grace by good works, tended more in the direction of saying that justifying grace comes only to those who sincerely repent. That seems to be the primary move taken, for instance, in the Saxon Visitation Articles in 1528 (I am beginning to think of them more and more as the cemetery of Reformation hopes). If the Old Adam cannot make it or earn grace by being good enough, at least he can do it by being sorry enough. So instead of mercifully putting the invalid out of misery, they chose to prolong the misery indefinitely by going to work on the psyche, setting up a means by which to *produce* the terrified conscience which, once given a little bit of grace, would supposedly be grateful enough subsequently to get back to the *real* business at hand, sanctification. Here reformation theology takes a subtle turn: Instead of being a solution to guilt it actually tries to produce guilt. The tendency was to dole out grace in bits—enough to assuage the "terrified conscience" perhaps, but not enough to harm the quest for morality.

What came under special attack in this kind of move was the *sola*, the *alone*, of "faith alone." Vinzenz Pfnür shows that various spokesmen objected, especially to the *sola*, and largely on so-called "practical" grounds. In the discussions which followed the presentation of the CA Eck demanded that the *sola* be left out because, he said, "The simple-minded will be led astray thereby, to think that faith alone, to the exclusion of grace and good works, justifies."[9] The Committee of Fourteen (seven Roman Catholics and seven Lutherans selected to mediate the differences) actually came to an agreement on a formulation that avoids the *sola* altogether [forgiveness takes places "through the *gratia gratum faciens* (grace making graced) and faith formally and actually (*formaliter*) understood, and through word and sacrament as through instrument and tool."[10]]. According to Pfnür, the basic and material reason why the *sola* was left out was to battle the misunderstanding of this formulation *among the people*, lest it lead to a false security and to an imaginary, presumptuous faith. "It makes for nastiness and rudeness, unruly and rash people,"[11] in the judgment of Eck.

Theologians like Pfnür undoubtedly think that a formulation which quietly buries the *sola* is the triumph of practical reason and ecumenical sanity. But such a formulation also betrays an extremely arrogant and patronizing position: One holds back on grace so as to make sure "all those simple folk" won't get the wrong idea! "Of course, it's all right for *us*, but not for 'the average layperson.' " One ought always to be suspicious whenever the "simple folk" or the much celebrated but nonexistent "ordinary laypeople" are used as an excuse for theological dishonesty, lack of effort, or sleight of hand. It is true (I believe it was Martin Kahler who said it) that it is part of the task of the systematic theologian to be the "defense attorney for the simple believer." But one should take that to mean just that: defense attorney, not attorney for the prosecution or, even worse, executioner! Of course if people have always been dominated by the legal language, they probably will get the wrong idea! One might even go so far as to say that *in those days* some more careful formulation, maybe even by way of compromise, was unavoidable. But can we rest content with that today, or even see it as the basis for ecumenical rapprochement, when the failure of such policy is evident? Those "simple folk," both Lutherans and Catholics, for whom the theologians were going to do such a great favor by robbing them of the *sola*, have long since left us now, to seek some graciousness, of whatever sort, elsewhere.

Burying the *sola* in the name of practical reason is moreover theologically a disaster because it simply helps once again to dampen the explosion which could blow some kind of hole in the walls of the legal stronghold. Timidity and lack of courage at just the crucial point puts one on the defensive and means that the hegemony of the legal language is prolonged and solidified. A theology which wants to hold nevertheless to justification by faith will then find itself in a rather embarrassing position. On the one hand it will be driven—as were the Lutherans—to ever more shrill and dogged insistence on justification by absolutely forensic decree. On the other hand it will be driven to defend itself against charges of being "soft on good works" by insisting on sanctification "too," albeit a sanctification that is absolutely distinguished and separated from justification—on the one hand to divorce it from all effects and on the other to insist on the effect as a necessary consequence. Perhaps one can say that the break in the continuity has to come somewhere. If it doesn't come in terms of death and life in the actual experience and life of the believer it comes in a rather *ersatz* fashion in the theology: One makes an absolute split between justification and sanctification! This means, usually, either that justification is isolated and one never gets much farther, or that it is left behind and one pays little attention to it at all—the important business is sanctification. But the general result then is that the legal rhetoric remains in force and dominates the Christian life. Justification is quickly given a lick and a promise so that one can get on to the "real" (practical, business at hand: sanctification, "progress" in "virtue" under "the law."

The problems within the Lutheran camp generated by this state of affairs are manifest already in the later confessional squabbles.

The attacks on the hegemony of legal terminology become more desperate, and by the same token, more futile. Antinomians like John Agricola, rebelling against a law used to "produce" repentance, take the tack of trying to banish law and its use from the church altogether. The difficulty with that is not, as most knee-jerk reaction has it, that it is just wrong, but that it is *impossible*. Only death is the end of the law, the death anticipated by faith in him who died and rose for us. The *attack* on the hegemony of the legal language was not wrong *per se*. The mistake, however, was to assume that *theologians* could end that hegemony by a tour de force—banning law from the church or erasing it from their books. To deal properly with the problem one can only make the move to the language of death and life and the reality that entails, which is exactly what Luther did in his Antinomian Disputations—writings of great interest and significance for this question that has been largely ignored (and not even translated into English). When one does not make the move to death-life language it is hardly much of an advance for the church to brand antinomianism as a desperately dangerous heresy in order to allow *nomism* silently to solidify its position. Antinomianism is often seen as the really dangerous and heinous heresy. One can hold all sorts of funny ideas about the Trinity, Christology, and Atonement and that won't bother anyone much, but to be antinomian—that is really serious business!

When nomism is thus tacitly encouraged, justification by faith only becomes more of a riddle and the problem never really gets solved. Indeed, one could say that antinomianism is forced underground only to surface again in very pious, covert forms. If one can't get rid of the law, one takes steps to tame it, cut it down to size, make it manageable.

What is antinomianism, after all? In essence, it is a *theological* attempt to bring the law to heel short of death by some kind of manipulation, overt and covert. If one can't end the law, one seeks to tone it down, to alter it, to apply it casuistically. Once that is understood it is clear that much very pious talk about "the third use of the law," and so forth, apart from consideration of the reality of the death and life in faith is actually a covert antinomianism. One disarms the law and makes it into a gentle guide which *we* use in our quest for virtue. Thus domesticated as the "house pet" of the pious, the law indeed remains but it has lost its teeth.[12]

Arguments for the "necessity" of good works illustrate the problem even more directly. Once one thinks exclusively in terms of the legal scheme and then superimposes justification by faith *sola*, and, indeed, moves even farther in the direction of pure forensic justification whenever threatened, it becomes exceedingly difficult to say why one should bother to do the "good works" demanded by that legal scheme at all. If justification is envisaged as a legal process and then one supposedly gets it all at the outset anyway by faith, the process itself seems "unnecessary." For the small price of "faith" one gets excused from the whole rest of the "process." If one is subsequently accused of being soft on good works, one has a hard time defending oneself without a sell-out. Just how "necessary" are good works if the "process" is unnecessary?

We have already noted some of the rather tentative and perhaps timid steps of the CA in this direction: Faith "should" produce good fruits and good works; faith "is bound to" do good works; good works "should and must" be done; and in one instance, even, "it is necessary" to do good works. Once such tentative essays are made it is only to be expected that someone will bite the bullet and blurt it all out: "We might as well say it and be honest. If it is necessary for faith to do good works, if faith is not faith without good works, if no one is saved without good works, then good works are necessary to salvation." So the Majorists. But that quite consequent and logical move, given the legal scheme, cannot but call for a last desperate counter-move to try once more to dislodge the hegemony of the legalist. So it was left to the earnest but bumbling old soul Nicolas von Amsdorf (patron saint of the dying Lutheran pastor we mentioned at the beginning of the chapter) to launch the crazy, kamikaze-like attack by actually having the guts to say that good works were not only not necessary, but detrimental to salvation!

On the face of it that is a theologically impossible and preposterous statement, of course. One might say, indeed, as the later confessional statements do, that the proposition is correct theologically, if people trust in good works to the extent that grace is excluded. Then it is true to say that such good works are detrimental to salvation. But one might go even farther and say that *in actual practice* the statement is truer than we might think. Given the legal scheme and a "forensic justification," one tends to reduce "good works" to the lowest common denominator of "doing something" at least—the little pious "somethings" that pass for "good works" and more often than not insulate us from doing anything more, anything significant. Amsdorf was right in most cases: "What passes for good work is detrimental to salvation!

The argument could not, of course, but call forth an attempt to mediate in terms of the given scheme. But that produced little more than a good deal of theological fine-tuning and word-smithing in the Formula of Concord which, while perhaps formally quite correct, doesn't have much affect on the real problem and allows everyone to go back to either the legalism or the lethargy they began with anyway.

Nothing shows more clearly the desperate need for the move to the idea of death and new life. If one is going to be at all serious about justification *sola fide*, about the *simul iustus et peccator;* if, whenever threatened, one is going to move even farther "to the right" and speak of absolutely forensic justification (and that move *is* essentially the right one) so that one comes up hard against the limit, against the fact that nothing is required because all is an unconditional gift, then the only way forward is to see that all that spells precisely death to the old, the end of the law and its hegemony, the end of the Old Adam and Eve and their desperate attempts to stay alive and find new possibility in the law. The way forward is not to hedge on the nothing, or qualify forensic justification with a little warmed-over mysticism, or withhold the *sola* lest the "simple" get the wrong idea, or "add" sanctification to keep people moral and domesticate the law. The only way forward is precisely *through* the nothing, through the death to new life. If there is a progress in the Christian life, it must be seen precisely as a progress driven by the justifying word which brings death and new life, a progress in dying to the old and being raised to the new. It is a situation where dying, we live.

This, I propose, is at bottom the kind of theology which lies behind the somewhat puzzling statements in the CA about the new obedience and good works. One can see this clearly by looking at the theology which produced it. When Luther wanted to talk about any sort of progress in the Christian life under the imputation of justification unconditionally, he grasped at formulations which stand usual understandings right on their head. The *simul iustus et peccator* makes it impossible to talk of some sort of moral progress in which one moves from one stage to another achieving a sort of perfection, and where every stage is the platform for the next leap. If that were the case, justification as an imputed, unconditional gift would make little sense. The higher one gets, the less grace one would need, until at last one could get along without it altogether. Justification by faith would be something like a temporary loan to cover the debtor until the debt was actually paid. Then the justification would no longer be needed. "Sanctification" and "good works" would be a matter of progressively paying off the debt, perhaps according to the popular slogan, *"Become* what you are!" where all the stress is usually on the *become* (you had better, or else!).

The *simul* makes all such schemes of progress impossible. The justification given is a total state, a complete, unconditional gift. From that point of view true sanctification is simply to "shut up and listen!" For there can be no *more* sanctification than where every knee bends and every mouth is silent before God, the only Holy One. And God is revered as the Holy One only where the sinner, the real sinner, stands still at the place where God enters the scene and speaks. That is the place where the sinner must realize that his or her way is at an end. Only those who are so grasped that they stand still here and confess to sin and give God the glory, only they are "sanctified." And there cannot be *more* sanctification than that! Whoever knows this knows that there is an end to the old, there is a death involved, and that being a Christian means ever and anew to be blasted by that divine lightning (for we always forget it) and to begin again. As Luther said, *"proficere, hoc est semper a novo incipere."* (To achieve means always to begin again anew).[13]

The "progress" of the Christian therefore, is the progress of one who has constantly to get used to the fact that we are justified totally by faith, constantly has somehow to "recover," so to speak, from that death blow to pride and presumption—or better, is constantly being raised from the tomb of all pious ambition to something quite new. The believer has to be renewed daily in that. The Old Being is to be daily drowned in repentance and raised in faith. The progress of the Christian life is not our movement toward the goal; it is the movement of the goal in upon us. The righteousness granted unconditionally is eschatological in character; it is the totality of the "Kingdom of God" moving in upon us. The sin to be attacked and abolished is not merely immorality and godlessness, but also pious presumption, the refusal to believe in God or his creation, always taking flight toward some spiritual dreamland. Sanctification cannot, therefore, mean that the ideas of moral progress blasted by the divine imputation of righteousness are now subtly smuggled back in under the table. The sin to be removed *is* precisely such understandings of progress. The justification is not a mere beginning point which can somehow be allowed to recede into the background while the supposed "real" business of sanctification takes front and center. The unconditional justification is the perpetual fountain, the constant source of whatever "righteousness" we may acquire. "Complete" sanctification is not the goal but the source of all good works. That, after all, is what it means to say, "Good works do not make a person good, but a good person does good works." The imputed, unconditional righteousness is not a temporary loan, or a legal fiction, but a power, indeed, "the power of God unto salvation." It attacks sin as a total state and will not relent until it has reduced all sin to nothing. It always attacks as a *whole*, as the unconditional word consigning the old to death and calling forth the new. When the confessions use statements like "Faith will bear fruit!" or "Faith is bound to bear fruit," that is what stands behind the statement.

Once that is clear, we should make no mistake about it: Sin and all its workings (religiosity as a profession) are to be abolished, and eventually will be abolished. But the abolition of sin, for Luther, was quite the opposite of a morally conceivable "process" of sanctification. In that sort of "process" the *person* remains more or less alive as a "substance" and only the "properties" are changed. A continuously existing subject always survives. There is no death and resurrection. One supposedly "puts off sin," Luther sarcastically remarks, as though one were peeling paint from a wall or taking heat from water.[14] Sanctification is like a coat of new paint applied after scraping off the old. But the old car itself remains the same and it would be hypocritical to call it "new." Justification *sola fide* is not a cosmetic process—"a new paint job." It does not, Luther insists, merely take the sin away and leave the moral person intact; rather it takes the person away from sin, heart, mind, soul, and affections. For Luther, sanctification involves a death and new life, not progress according to some moral scheme.

> Human righteousness . . . seeks first of all to remove and to change the sins and *to keep man intact;* this is why it is not righteousness but hypocrisy. Hence as long as there is *life* in man and as long as he is not *taken* by renewing grace to be changed totally, no efforts of his can prevent him from being subject to sin and the law.[15]

Sanctification viewed as progress in "partialities" or mere changing of "properties" would be nothing but hypocrisy. For justification means death and new life.

We need only to recall familiar statements from the Small Catechism and elsewhere to establish this:

> What does such baptizing with water signify?
> Answer: It signifies that the old Adam in us, together with all sins and evil lusts, should be drowned by daily sorrow and repentance and be put to death, and that the new man should come forth daily and rise up, cleansed and righteous, to live forever in God's presence.[16]

> Baptism . . . is simply the slaying of the old Adam and the resurrection of the new man, both of which must continue in us our whole life long. Thus a Christian life is nothing else than a daily Baptism, once begun and ever continued. For we must keep at it incessantly, always purging out whatever pertains to the old Adam, so that whatever belongs to the new may come forth.[17]

In the passage from *The Babylonian Captivity of the Church* to which we referred earlier Luther insists that this death is not merely allegorical or a symbol for the purging of sin (merely a change of "properties") but *real*, and then goes on to say:

> Neither does sin completely die, nor grace completely rise, until the sinful body that we carry about in this life is destroyed, as the Apostle says in the same passage (Rom. 6:6–7). For as long as we are in the flesh, the desires of the flesh stir and are stirred. For this reason, *as soon as we begin to believe, we also begin to die* to this world and live to God in the life to come, so that faith is truly a death and a resurrection, that is, it is that spiritual baptism into which we are submerged and from which we rise.[18]

There is a kind of progress, a kind of growth spoken of; one cannot mistake that. But it is a progress in dying to the old and being raised in the new.

But what does such talk mean? It means simply that under the power of the absolutely unconditional decree—"I love you, you are mine, I will never let you go; you are just for Jesus' sake"— we might begin at least to love God from the heart. When we simply listen to him, that is, we might begin to love him and bear good fruit. Faith born of the unconditional decree, a decree made in spite of everything, will begin to see the truth of the human condition, the reality and totality of human sin in the pursuit of both vices *and* virtues. Such a faith will begin to see the fantastic magnitude of the divine act, the miracle of a God who *nevertheless* does business with sinners, and actually begin, however hesitatingly and falteringly, to love God from the heart, to hate sin and the self of sin, and to hope for that righteousness which it knows full well it can never attain by any known scheme of moral or virtuous progress—the righteousness of faith. Such a faith *is* a death and the beginning of resurrection precisely because it is a belief in the speaking of God which defies all empirical evidence—faith in the promise. It is a faith which once having heard might cry to God out of the depths: "Wretched man that I am, who will deliver me? . . ." and actually begin to "hunger and thirst after righteousness."

When Luther and the Confessions speak in this vein they are

talking about actual affection: love, hope, hatred of sin, and "the body of death," not about theological abstractions. That is what Luther meant when he said that the person is being taken away from sin, not sin somehow purged from the person. The radical nature of the divine imputation brings a death and resurrection. The person is "transported" to use a modern idiom, taken away from sin when the radical nature of the justifying act sets the totally just (the *totus iustus*) over against the complete sinner (the *totus peccator*) and begins to kindle the first beginnings of actual hope and love where before there had been only hypocrisy and despair. For then the great commandment, "Thou shalt love . . ." begins to become a reality. It begins to sound not just as a demand, a law, but as a promise: "You shall love, you will love one day, for I love you unconditionally. One day the last barrier will fall and you will be mine completely! You can bet your life on it!" Justification, election, predestination, all those things may sound frightening now, but one day you will see and whisper 'Amen'!"

That is what the confession means when it says, "When through faith the Holy Spirit is given, the *heart* is moved to do good works. Before that, when it is without the Holy Spirit, the heart is too weak."[19] Or again: "Without faith and without Christ human nature and human strength are much too weak to do good works, call upon God, have patience in suffering, love one's neighbor, diligently engage in callings which are commanded, . . . Such great and genuine works cannot be done without the help of Christ."[20] It is a matter of the "heart," of the real affections, a matter of the spontaneity that flows from having heard at last the "I love you" that has absolutely no strings attached. Good works, according to the confessional position, flow spontaneously from justification.

It is often said that the Reformers were naive in this view, not taking seriously sanctification and the grim reality of gritting one's teeth, disciplining the body, and slogging along. That is not true. That problem arose only later when the explosion had long been forgotten and everyone had lost courage—"chickened out" by degrees—and finally gone on the defensive vis-à-vis schemes of law, morality, virtue, and progress. When everyone resorts to defending themselves and insulating themselves *against* the explosion, it is no wonder that nothing happens. Luther's famous words from his *Preface to Romans* bears repeating:

> Faith is a divine work in us which changes us and births us anew out of God (John 1:13), and kills the old Adam, makes us into entirely different people from the heart, soul, mind, and all powers, and brings the Holy Spirit with it. Oh it is a living, busy, active, mighty thing, this faith, so it is impossible that it should not do good. It does not ask if good works should be done, but before one asks, has done them and is always active. Whoever, though, does not do such work is a faithless person, peeking and poking about for faith and good works not knowing what either faith or good works are, who putters in much verbiage about faith and good works.[21]

Faith simply does good works naturally and spontaneously. It is not naive to insist on that—*if* one has any inkling at all of what the explosion of justification is! To say that it is naive is more a reflection on the cynicism of the speaker than on the Reformers who held that view. The scriptures and the Reformation have too much invested in this to have it dismissed by epigoni who no longer have any conception of the faith of which they speak. If there is no spontaneity, then there is no light at the end of the tunnel at all and the darkness in which we dwell is that of the tomb.

Faith doesn't *ask* about good works, but does them without all the theological fuss and bother. Good works are works done in faith, the faith which has simply gotten over looking at itself and its "progress" and begun to look at the neighbor. Good works should be quite as natural and spontaneous as a parent running to pick up and comfort a child who has fallen and gotten hurt. One doesn't stop to think about it. ("Let me see now, should I do this or shouldn't I? Is it necessary?"); one doesn't even worry about whether it is a good work or not—one just does it. And after it is over, one forgets about it completely. That is what good works are like. They are probably those works we have forgotten all about.

Perhaps that old pastor who said he couldn't remember doing a good work in his life was on to something! After all, "When you give alms, sound no trumpet before you, as the hypocrites . . . that they may be praised by men. . . . But when you give alms, do not let your left hand know what your right hand is doing, so that your alms may be in secret; and your Father who sees in secret will reward you" (Matt. 6: 2ff). If there is such a thing as growth in the Christian life, it is growth in that sort of thing—growth in grace, in forgetting oneself, in being grasped by the fact that in the end we can be saved only by grace alone. When we get that through our heads and hearts the way is open for good works.

So we can return to the perennial question: "But we have to do something, don't we?" That, you see, is no longer the question. Rather the question has become: "What are you going to do, now that you don't *have to* do anything?" "What's the matter, don't you *want to?*" "How can you who have died to sin still live in it?" For all the world we act like a lover looking at the beloved on the wedding night and asking, "But I *have to* do something, don't I?" The only appropriate answer to that question is, "If that's the way you feel about it, forget it! Get out of here!" "To him who has, more will be given, but from him who has not even what he has will be taken away." (Mark 4:24).

So all the language about the "necessity" of good works is more or less beside the point. It is of the nature of faith to do good works just as it is of the nature of love to love and care to care, of the parent to pick up and comfort that hurt child. To say that is not naive; it is the expression of confidence and hope. Of course the Reformers were quite aware that we don't come by such spontaneity easily and that it is only very imperfect in us at best. But that is no reason to kill it altogether. The tender flower can only be watered and cared for by the constant application of unconditional justification. *Semper incipere!*

The reformers of course always had back-up protection against anyone who hadn't really caught the vision but simply wanted to exploit the *sola fide:* If you don't *want to* do good works, if the spontaneity is not there, then the law will see to it that you do them anyway. To some extent at least you will *have to* do good works. There is always the law—the judge, the jury, the hangman—as the Reformers said, "the power of the sword." But such power is—strictly speaking—someone else's business, someone else's game, not directly the church's. It is the game of the "secular authorities" —the "left hand." If you don't want to love and care for that hurt child there are people and laws whose business it is to see to it that you *have to*, to see to it that you carry out your responsibilities whether you like it or not. But that is often a rather grim business and all such "have too" affairs should not simply be confused or identified with doing good works or sanctification. To be realistic, this side of the eschaton we shall no doubt have to say that in our actual deeds there is something of a mixture of the *have to* and the *want to*, maybe even a good deal more of the former than of the latter. But we must not lose sight of the hope, the vision, inspired by the absolutely unconditional promise. For in the end, that alone will survive—true sanctification.

But, we must ask at last: What are we to do, now that we don't *have to* do anything? In the Confessional statements there are some interesting assertions about good works that we have not yet explored. The Reformers say they have been falsely accused of forbidding good works (no doubt a reference to statements from the early days in which they denied the place of good works in justification, the merit scheme—the so-called "polemical exaggerations"), and then they usually go on to say that even though good works do not justify, we must do "all such good works as God has commanded, but do them for God's sake and not place our trust in them"; do them in order that "we may do God's will and glorify him." The Confessions generally make some sort of judgment about the *kind* of good works we are to do. They claim that their teachers (the Reformers) have given "good and profitable accounts and instructions concerning true Christian estates and works," something, they judge, which has not been hitherto since sermons and instruction have been concerned with "childish and useless works" —rosaries, the cult of saints, monasticism, pilgrimages, fasts, and holy days. Without faith, they aver, we are too weak to do what they call "great and genuine" works: call upon God, have patience in suffering, love one's neighbor, diligently engage in callings which are commanded, render obedience, and avoid evil lusts.

Statements of this sort are to be carefully regarded since they are the answer to our new question: What are you going to do, now that you don't *have to* do anything? The faith born of the unconditional promise finds a new world opening up—in which God's creation is given back as sheer gift—the world of the other, the world of the neighbor, where "great and genuine" works are to be done *because it is God's will*. Once one has been cured of all heaven-storming ambitions one suddenly finds God's *creation* to care about and for. The works are to be "great and genuine"; they are to be a piece of real coin, not the "childish and useless" sort of thing. That is, they are to be works in and for the world, works done for others in our callings, the "Christian estates," not works done for the self in its quest for holiness, its dream of moral progress and virtue. The unconditional gift opens up an entirely different view of God's will and God's commandments. What we are to do, now that we don't have to do anything for ourselves, is *God's* will.

The Reformation understanding of the will of God and the commandments is premised on the belief that the commandments of God *do not* lead one on a quest for personal holiness and virtue, but precisely into the world of the neighbor. If you look at a writing like Luther's "On Monastic Vows" you will discover the main point to be that if one really follows God's commandments, one is led into the world of the family, the neighbor, and the world, not into the area of self-chosen "holy" works. To die to the old, the self, is to begin to live to the world of the other, where God's commandments take us.

The point of justification by faith is not to foster a relaxation of ideals or reduce everything to the lowest common denominator of what is generally attainable in daily life. The point is rather that the so-called "religious" and "pious" works are simply self-chosen and thus not the will of God. God, for instance does not command poverty or chastity as some sort of ideal for those who want to be truly holy. Vows of poverty and chastity, Luther felt, do not necessarily mean obeying God's will since they are mostly self-chosen for the sake of one's own holiness. One might, of course, want to question today whether that necessarily is always the case, but the theological point must be taken seriously—that the true contest here is between works chosen for one's own holiness and works commanded by God for the welfare of the neighbor. That is what stands behind the Confessional assertion that we must do such good works as are commanded by God.

God's will, God's commandments lead us into this new world—the world of the other. Whoever has a lust for one's own holiness, Luther says, will never care much for the commandments of God. Because the commandments of God take one away from the quest for one's own holiness into the world. The commandment doesn't lead to spiritual isolation on inaccessible mountaintops, but it might well lead to washing dirty diapers! Living by the commandments is therefore quite the opposite from the quest for one's own holiness. It means incarnating what *God* wants in and for his world. The new being, the being who comes through death to life is to be incarnated in "down to earth" fashion in the concrete calling of the Christian. For this being, the will of God is no longer an enemy, but a true friend. Make no mistake about it: for Luther, the Reformers, the Confessions, the law of God is to be and will be fulfilled. It cannot be fulfilled, however, except one be grasped by the unconditional decree, going through death to life. Dying, we live—by faith. Faith in life is exercised in death: faith not in some pious never-never land, the quintessence of our religious ambitions or self-preservation, but faith in God's creation, where his will is done *for his sake* until he at last rings down the curtain and perfects all things.

4

FREEDOM TO LIVE

Freedom! Just to speak the word is to enter the holy of holies of what we have come to call the modern world. Freedom is the goal of all our striving, the pot of gold at the end of the rainbow. Everyone wants it: political freedom, economic freedom, psychological freedom, sexual freedom, religious freedom, racial freedom, freedom of speech, freedom of the press, free trade, free markets, academic freedom, freedom from fear, freedom from want and hunger, and the list could go on endlessly. Anyone who feels put under any undue restraint or inhibition by almost anything whatsoever wants "liberation."

In spite of that desperate desire, however, freedom seems to be an extremely elusive goal. "Man is born free," said Rousseau long ago, "and everywhere he is in chains." That opening sentence of the *Social Contract* seems as true to many today as it was in the eighteenth century when it was first written. Every advance in freedom on one front seems to bring new forms of slavery on another. Economic and political freedom for some only seem to bring slavery and exploitation for others. There are signs even that the idea itself is becoming a bit jaded. B. F. Skinner, the famous behavioral psychologist has suggested to the horror of most, in *Beyond Freedom and Dignity*,[1] that if civilization is to survive we can no longer afford the rhetoric of freedom. It no longer works. All the incentives to get people to behave properly in freedom no longer function. Heaven does not attract and hell does not threaten. In many instances, not even money, he says, can induce us to behave properly. That (for better or for worse) is probably less true now than it was in the early seventies when Skinner wrote

61

on the topic. He maintains the theory in his book that behavior will have to be programmed by scientific means, that is, by the principles of behavorial science, to insure the future of the race. Among the young as well, the supposed champions of freedom, there are traces of disenchantment. "Freedom's just another word for nothin' left to lose," sings Janis Joplin in "Me and Bobby McGee." When Bobby leaves her, "lookin' for a home," he's free, but that's just "nothing"—"nothin' left to lose." It is little wonder that many youth, having looked this emptiness—this "nothin' left to lose"—in the face, have fled frightened into the bondage of fanatic religious sects of one sort or another.

So it is useful for us now and again to look at the Confessional teaching about freedom and to attempt unravelling what it is all about. Perhaps particularly against the background of our own problems in this country with questions of predestination, election, and freedom it might be useful to take another look—if we can do so without rancor and needlessly opening old wounds. Here again it seems clear that we shall not be able systematically to unravel the snarl of predestination and human responsibility unless we take into account the fact of death and life. There is no possibility of solving the problem of an active electing and predestinating God standing over against a continuously existing, active subject caught in the scheme of the conditional, legal metaphor. When an active electing God confronts a continuously existing active subject over the question of ultimate destiny, one of them will eventually have to give way. We might, of course, attempt hairsplitting compromises to save a bit of both, but that won't work. Either God or the creature will become fictional. If we try to preserve the continuity of the subject, even to the smallest degree —effecting whatever compromise we can—the electing God dies a slow, systematic death. And from one point of view at least, that has been the story of modern theology. On the other hand, if we try to assert the primacy and place of the electing God, then the subject is gradually reduced to nothing—some kind of subservient, timorous church mouse, scared of its own dogmatic shadow. As an astute observer of the election controversy put it, "You cure the disease, but you kill the patient!"

Of course! It does comes to that—to a matter of death. But somehow we have to get to life! Kant saw the issue clearly long ago when he said that if there is such a thing as historical revelation, so that faith in this historical revelation is able to make new persons of us from the ground up, then everything connected with such a revelation and faith would resolve itself to an unconditional decree of God: "He has mercy on whom he wills, and whom he wills he hardens." Which, Kant says, ". . . taken according to the letter is the *salto mortale* (the death leap) of human reason."[2]

With Kant, virtually the whole modern world resolutely turned its back on such a death leap—no doubt because it could see no hope in resurrection. So instead of facing the question of our own death theologically we have been busily trying to do a job on God. We have, so to speak, been trying to put him in his place, to cut him down to size. It has all happened before, of course. When God came to us, we put him on a cross. We killed him once. He has died for us once, for all—for all time, for all people. There is no need to do it again. As Paul could have put it, Christ Jesus, having died once to sin, dies no more. He is risen from the dead and lives eternally. The job is finished. Now, to put it bluntly, it is our turn. Whoever would save his or her life shall lose it; whoever loses his or her life for Jesus' sake shall find it. It is a matter of death and life.

In theological terms, what we have overlooked in our hassles about human responsibility and divine election is just the fact of death and life. On the systematic level many of our problems would be solved if we could say that the person who is bound, unfree, rejected, and to be consigned to death is the old being, while the one who arises from the dead in faith is the new being, elect of God—free. The new being emerges from the waters of Baptism to say "amen" to God, the Almighty Creator of heaven and earth, the electing one. If we could just surrender our own continuity as the old being, we might then learn to find our destiny and continuity *extra nos* in the one who rose from the dead. We would find our continuity precisely in the Triune God—carried by the faith that the God who created us is also our redeemer and the giver of new life in the Spirit.

Theologically, systematically, we ought to be able to see that.

The break in continuity would solve the systematic problem. But, of course, the way from a neat systematic distinction of that sort to an actual resolution in our own lives is long. The gate is narrow and the road is straight. Paul, apparently, could say it: For me to live is Christ and to die is gain. But who of us can say that without a shudder? Luther himself has certainly taught us that we can't substitute dogmatic or systematic distinctions for actual experience. So we have to descend into the maelstrom of the discussion about free will to see how things actually are with us. The actual and existential questions may only be aggravated by the dogmatic distinctions. When we face this discontinuity in actuality the questions are no doubt real cries of protest and agony. "Do you mean to say I don't have a choice?" "God doesn't violate human personality, does he?" "We can at least say no, can't we?" "We aren't puppets, are we?" "What of human responsibility?" And so on. All the questions have one central content: What will happen to *me* if I fall into the hands of the living God?

So with all the questions buzzing about once again, let us look at the Confessional statement and develop something of the theology which lies behind it. In Article XVIII entitled "Freedom of the Will" we find the following (from the Latin version):

> Our churches teach that man's will has some liberty for the attainment of civil righteousness and for the choice of things subject to reason. However, it does not have the power, without the Holy Spirit, to attain the righteousness of God—that is, spiritual righteousness—because natural man does not perceive the gifts of the Spirit of God (1 Cor. 2:14), but this righteousness is wrought in the heart when the Holy Spirit is received through the Word.[3]

That is the basic statement. Then the article concludes with a quotation ascribed to St. Augustine to demonstrate that the position is "no novelty" (German version) but standard Christian tradition. The quote is important and helpful enough to bear repeating:

> In Book III of his *Hypognosticon*, Augustine said these things in so many words: "We concede that all men have a free will which enables them to make judgments according to reason. However, this does not enable them, without God, to begin or (much less) to accomplish anything in those things which pertain to God, for it is

only in acts of this life that they have freedom to choose good or evil. By 'good' I mean the acts which spring from the good in nature, that is, the will to labor in the field, will to eat and drink, will to have a friend, will to clothe oneself, will to build a house, will to marry, will to keep cattle, will to learn various useful arts, or will to do whatever good pertains to this life. None of these exists without the providence of God; indeed, it is from and through him that all these things come into being and are. On the other hand, by 'evil' I mean such things as the will to worship an idol, will to commit murder," and so forth.[4]

Now what lies behind that statement? What does it mean? The words reflect, of course, what Luther had said in *The Bondage of Will* in attempting to define the sense in which one could properly use the term "free will":

If we do not want to drop this term altogether—which would really be the safest and most Christian thing to do—we may still in good faith teach people to use it to credit man with "free will" in respect, not of what is above him, but of what is below him. That is to say, man should realize that in regard to his money and possession he has a right to use them, to do or to leave undone, according to his own "free will"—though that very "free will" in overruled by the free will of God alone, according to his own pleasure. However, with regard to God and in all that bears on salvation or damnation, he has no "free will," but is a captive, prisoner and bond-slave, either to the will of God, or to the will of Satan.[5]

What shall we make of this? At the outset, of course, it is necessary to recall that when we join discussion about freedom or bondage of the will we are entering one of the most sensitive areas of Reformation theology. Catholics and even most Protestants become uneasy and upset when this position on free will and its correlative idea of divine election, predestination, and necessity is pushed very hard. This is another one of the instances in which we have to deal with one of the so-called "polemical exaggerations" of the early Reformation days, especially some of the early statements of Luther—another area, that is to say, where we are faced once again with the crucial question: Are we to retreat, put the damper on the explosion, and go on the defensive or is there a way ahead?

What especially rankled Roman Catholic theologians of Luther's day were some of his statements about divine necessity. Luther could say when pressed that God rules all things by necessity and that therefore free will was actually just a word, a mere title, without any reality.[6] Not only does this seem to cancel human responsibility, but it also appears to make God the cause of sin and evil. This, of course, was extremely offensive to "catholic" ears. And once again, contemporary Catholic interpreters tend to see the Augsburg Confession as something of a corrective to those supposed early excesses since it refrains from rash statements about divine necessity and also in the article immediately following (XIX) tries to exculpate God from being a cause of sin.[7] Sin, it is said, is caused by the will of the wicked (Latin version), or by the perverted will (German version), which turns away from God to evil "If not aided by God . . . "(Latin) or " . . . as soon as God withdraws his support . . . "(German). Whether blame is to be laid on God for "withdrawing his support," is, of course, a question not pursued! At any rate, Catholics seem pleased with such statements and interpret them as a "correction" to earlier supposedly rash and unguarded "polemical exaggerations."

So to interpret the matter, and thus to have done with it is, however, something of a mistake. It is perhaps true that the Augsburg Confession, together with the Formula of Concord, has already taken the wrong turn towards obscuring the Reformation position in the very fact that an article is offered on "free" will instead of on the "bondage" of the will.[8] There is nothing particularly new to be said when one comes at the question from the angle of free will. One tends only to compromise the point. So it is not strange that Catholic theologians after Augsburg found nothing in particular to argue with in the article itself. It is also true that Melanchthon himself, in his own theology, moved slowly but steadily in the direction of compromising the Reformation position on the bondage of the will. But one cannot take Melanchthon's movement here as normative, nor as the key to interpreting what Lutherans as a whole have understood the Augsburg Confession to be saying. One must interpret the article on free will against the background of the earlier theology, and especially against the background of those so-called "polemical exaggerations." For here, as elsewhere, the key to understanding the position is hidden precisely in those "exaggerations." We must forge ahead if we are to break any new ground for understanding. To interpret the Confession as a culmination of a move toward compromise and corrective is a fatal error.

So what stands behind Article XVIII? First of all, as far as the (theo-) logic of it is concerned, the Article is simply the consequence of the Reformation understanding of justification by faith and divine predestination. Justification *sola fide* and predestination are simply two sides of the same coin. If justification is an absolutely unconditional decree, if God does it all by himself on his own initiative in such a way that it brings death to the old unbeliever and resurrection to the new in faith, then it comes as the result of his decision, his judgment. He is there "before" us. He is prior. He, as the theological word has it, "pre-" destines. "Indeed, within any Reformation theology, a doctrine of predestination is merely the article of justification stated with respect to God."[9] Anyone who takes God seriously at all has to reckon with some sort of predestination.[10] It simply goes with the business of being precisely *God*.

Furthermore, this assertion of divine predestination carries with it the corollary of divine necessity which is also so offensive to our ears. If the justifying deed is unconditional, putting to death the old and really bringing a new future, it must therefore be set in the all-encompassing will of this predestining God. It must speak of the outcome of the entire created enterprise without remainder. "In terms of God, if the gospel-promise is unconditional and true, the will which is real in that promise must encompass every event whatever. Whether we like it or not, it is a strict implication of the doctrine of justification: whatever happens, happens by God's will."[11] Justification *sola fide* brings with it, that is to say, just that doctrine of necessity, even those "polemical exaggerations" which so offend us if it is at all seriously held. That is simply the "theo-logic" of the matter.

But what does this say about human freedom? Given such a position, does it even make sense to say, as the Augsburg Confession does, that we have some freedom for the "attainment of civil righteousness and for the choice of things subject to reason?" Wouldn't one rather have to draw the conclusion that we have no freedom at all? If God rules all things by necessity, how can we be left any freedom of any sort? We, it would seem, can be nothing more than "puppets." That is where the "logic" of the matter would seem to lead.

So to proceed according to the apparent "logic" of the matter, however, would be seriously to miss the point because that logic is just not true. The Reformation and Confessional position is not a theory about the "logic" of the matter, it is an attempt to describe what is actually the case, an attempt to talk about actual experience, the way things actually are. It is an attempt to talk about actual, not theoretical, freedom and un-freedom. The fact is that whatever metaphysic or logic we may hold, we *are* free to do a lot of things. Strictly speaking, being theoretically a determinist, for instance, puts no real restraints on what I might or might not do with my life, just as being a libertarian does not liberate me or give me any more real options. Aside from the fact that such positions may affect my psyche or my mind-set, they don't necessarily place any actual restraints on what I can or cannot do, or open any new possibilities. We tend to do what we want regardless of—or often in spite of—our "metaphysics." That is what it means to say as Luther did, that we have free will in those things which are "below us," or as the Confession has it, "for the attainment of civil righteousness and for the choice of things subject to reason." It is a simple fact of experience. On that level, as a piece of graffiti I saw on the walls of Wellesley College library some time ago put it, "The only thing you need to know to be free is that nothing is stopping you!" Not even the most ironclad logical determinism can stop you! On that level the irrefutable answer to the perpetual question, "We aren't puppets, are we?" is simply, "Look, no strings!"

So we are actually quite free in those things "below us," free for the attainment of "civil righteousness"—doing good, even, in a general philanthropic sense. As the statement in the Confession put it, we are free to perform acts which "spring from the good in nature," to labor in the field, eat and drink, will to have a friend, will to clothe oneself, will to build a house, will to marry, to keep cattle, to learn various useful arts, or do whatever good pertains to this life. One might add, we can even will to go to church, to become religious, to be very moral and pious. Nothing really stops us from all that. It is "below us."

There is, of course something that *could* stop us and that would be sheer physical impossibility, superior force, accident, or perhaps natural catastrophe, untimely death. That is what Luther means when he adds that though we are free in those things below us, that very free will is "overruled" by the free will *of God alone*, according to his own pleasure. The only thing that can stop us in those things below, is if God himself should decide actually to intervene and bring our efforts to naught. Thus also the Confession approves the statement in the quotation attributed to Augustine, "None of these things exists without the providence of God; indeed, it is from and through him that all these things come into being and are." Divine providence makes this sort of freedom possible and it alone can nullify it. That is just the way things are.

Now, if that is the case, the other part of the statement that we are not free (do not have free choice) in those things "above us," or as the Confession puts it, human will " . . . does not have the power, without the Holy Spirit, to attain the righteousness of God—that is, spiritual righteousness—because natural man does not perceive the gifts of the Spirit of God" (1 Cor. 2:14), that part of the Confession is meant equally to be a statement of fact, a confession about the way things actually are, and not a theoretical deduction from certain principles. It means that there *is* something we just cannot do without the Holy Spirit, something we are absolutely not able to do. That something is reconciliation with God.

Now the question is, why are we not able to do it? If nothing, except such things as accident, death, superior force, or natural catastrophe, can stop us from doing what we will in earthly things, what in all creation can stop us from reconciling ourselves to God if we want to, or at least making some little contribution thereto? We all will admit that we aren't the best of saints, but "we do the best we can, don't we?" The flesh is indeed weak and we all get dragged down to some degree or another, but the spirit, at least, is willing—if only a tiny bit now and then. What is to stop us? Is not the "spirit" free in spite of physical and fleshly hindrances? Why are we not able to do this one thing?

Is God the reason? Is it because God predestines and rules all things by necessity that we are not able to do as we please in those things which are "above us?" This is the way we most often imagine the matter. We hear all the things about predestination and necessity and we immediately jump to the conclusion that God is some sort of transcendent "big meany" who makes it impossible for us to do the things we so desperately want. God frustrates our wills by imposing his, willy-nilly.

We have an incurable tendency to falsify matters. That is the problem. When we look away from things below to that which is above, we tend to think of ourselves (at least) potentially as spiritual athletes, just lusting to make "God's team." Our only problem is that we keep breaking the training rules now and then, or perhaps we aren't quite good enough or big enough. "Down deep," "spiritually" we really want to do it, will to do it, but the "flesh" keeps getting in the way. When we hear of divine predestination and election that simply adds one more injustice to the whole difficult matter. God is pictured as one who adds insult to injury by frustrating our desires. All our resentment comes pouring out in the incessant question: "But . . . , but, we do have a choice, don't we?" "After all, God does respect human personality, doesn't he?"

The fact is that the whole picture we tend to paint is incredibly false. Why can't we do it? Because at bottom we do not *want* to. When we come to those things which are above, our wills are *bound* by some other faith, some other vision, and thus will not—not want to—attend to the things of God. That is why it is a mistake already for the Confession even to offer an article on "free will." The article should have been on the *bound* will. For the question is not that of the degree to which our wills are free to do what they want within physical limits or whatever limits may or may not be set by God's will. The question is not one of what is "left over" for our freedom after all the prior and more powerful forces have had their way. The question is rather one of what we have done with the freedom we have been given. The question has to do with the way things are, the actual state and commitment of the will in its alienation from God. The Confessional and Reformation point is not that we don't have wills, nor is it that these wills are somehow frustrated by a transcendent bully or puppeteer, but rather that we have sold ourselves into a slavery from which there is no escape. And we have done this quite willingly. We are bound to do it. We will to do it. We cannot reconcile ourselves to God because we don't want to. That is the depth of the seriousness of the case. It is not without reason that the Confession at this point quotes 1 Cor. 2:14: "Natural man does not perceive the gifts of the Spirit of God." We just don't see. We labor under an incredibly false picture of ourselves. As Luther put it:

> . . . The scripture sets before us a man who is not only bound, wretched, captive, sick and dead, but who, through the operation of Satan his Lord, adds to his other miseries that of blindness, so that he believes himself to be free, happy, possessed of liberty and ability, whole and alive.[12]

The assertion that we cannot reconcile ourselves to God because we do not *want* to needs, no doubt, some explication. But once again, it is simply a matter of looking at the way things are. We are not free with respect to those things which are above us, that is, we are not free with respect to God. Why not? Because he is above us. He is, after all, God, and we don't like that. We are at best ambivalent about God. On the one hand we like the idea of an eternal source and anchor of being, an eternal fount of love, truth, beauty, and goodness. But on the other hand there are all the other things that go with the job which we don't like at all: almightiness, immutability, absoluteness, omniscience, omnipresence, not to speak of providence, predestination, and election. We have a great deal of trouble with such things because they don't seem to leave us any "freedom" at all. In all that he is "above" me; he is *God;* he is "number one" and that is precisely the problem.

But we must attend quite carefully to what it means to say I have no freedom or better; over against this God who is above me I am bound. This bondage or lack of freedom is not, for the Reformation, the result of a deduction from God's almightiness or immutability. It is rather the result of our *reaction* to the very idea of God, or recoil from the idea of God's "godness," his being "above us." In other words, it is not because God rules all things immutably or by necessity that I am unfree—bound in the Reformation sense—but rather it is because *I can't take the idea* of God at all that I recoil in horror and fall back on my own resources. We must remember that we are dealing with the *bondage* of the will, not a theoretical determinism of the will. In those things which are above me I am not free, not because I am somehow secretly or mysteriously controlled like a puppet on an invisible string, but because of what I have done with my freedom, because I simply am bound. The die has been cast. I can't be reconciled, because I don't *want* to be! What happens is this. When I come up against the idea of God, one who by definition is absolute, one who in addition is the Almighty Creator who disposes over all things by his providence, predestination, and election, I am, in my alienation, *bound* to react in a certain way. The *logic* of the case tells me that God determines everything, including my own destiny. In the face of that, what can *I* do? I can only say no, in one way or another. Frightened by what seems to be the logic of the case, I simply *assert* my own freedom so as to have something to say about my own responsibility and destiny. Given the fact that I don't know God—really, I don't know what he is up to but have only heard about him and drawn some logical conclusions about him—given the fact, as Luther would have put it, that God is hidden, I must take my destiny into my own hands. I must claim at least a little bit of freedom. We must note here that under the circumstances that is something I *must* do; I am bound to do it because I don't want to do anything else. I must say to God, in effect, "God, I don't know what you are up to. I can't trust you with your godness. Therefore I must take my destiny into my own hands, because I think it would be better that way." After all, "We do have a choice, don't we?" "I think it would be better if I decided such matters." "You can be almighty, God, in everything except what concerns my ultimate destiny!"

In this light, the assertion of free will is not really a logical position at all. It is a recoil from God, a defense mechanism against God. At bottom it is a faith *sui generis,* a faith in myself in defiance of God. In its most blatant form it means simply that we think things would be better and safer if *we* decide who is to inhabit his eternal kingdom than if *he* does.

The problem is bondage—a bondage which springs from our desperate alienation. That is what it means to say we are unreconciled. I am not forced by some mysterious power behind the scenes to do something I don't want to do. The problem is rather that I do just what I want. Indeed, the problem is that I can do only what I want and nothing more. I am bound to do it and thus I sell myself into slavery and I cannot escape—not without the Holy Spirit: "I cannot by my own reason or strength believe . . . "

"We do have a choice, don't we?" Now perhaps we can begin to see why the best answer to that persistent question is "Yes, indeed, we have a choice, but the problem is that we have already made it. The die has been cast. Our answer to God is 'no.' " We are simply not free in those things which are above us.

Our problem is bondage, bondage of the will. And the problem is compounded by the fact that in seeking to escape the logic of God we leap out of the frying pan into the fire. Frightened by God's godness, his absoluteness, immutability, predestination, and all those "horrible masks" we think to escape and bring matters under control by reaching some sort of compromise. We seek, most often, to limit God's absoluteness in some fashion or to make convenient distinctions which allow us some room to operate, at least some little bit of freedom. But to do so is to run from a theoretical bondage into an actual one. Fearing determinism (a theoretical loss of freedom), we attempt to achieve salvation ourselves by the exercise of the "freedom" we have claimed. We jump from theoretical bondage into actual bondage under the law. For now the word is: See to it yourself! Seeking to make it by the use of our "freedom," we are now found "under the law." Out of the frying pan into the fire! We sell ourselves into bondage, and there is no way out. We are afflicted with a fundamental disaffection, an alienation, a bondage.

What then is the cure? What is the answer? Once again, we can find our way forward only if we see that it is a matter of death and life. There is no way to get through to the bound, alienated, disaffected will directly. The will which is really bound but *thinks* itself free will only gobble up everything in its own self-serving machinery, however pious. God will be pictured as one who comes hat-in-hand offering this "free will" a "choice." (After all God doesn't violate human personality, does he?) We will live (temporarily at least) by falsifying accounts—looking upon ourselves as those spiritual athletes whose only problem is "weakness" or a few lapses in the training rules now and then. There is no way to cure such a patient. The trouble is the sickness unto death. So death and new life are the only cure. We see here the deepest reason for the theology of justification by faith alone, justification by the divine unconditional decree, indeed, by divine predestination. Only if the one who is above us makes an actual move to help us do we have a chance.

That is exactly the point of the doctrine of predestination—God makes the move to come to us. It is not a doctrine about what God might or might not be up to in heaven, but what he is actually about here on earth. It is a question of what he *actually* does. He cannot come to us directly, so he comes to die for us. He chose so to do—to reconcile the world unto himself—all by himself! That is the point of what was called the theology of the cross. God comes, as Luther said, "under the form of opposites,"—just the opposite of what the rational "free will" might want or expect. He does not come as the great or obvious king asking for a choice, but as the humble, suffering, despised, and rejected outcast who is beaten, spit upon, and "wasted" as one quite superfluous to the way we want things run here. There is no way to get through to the disaffected will directly, so life can only come through death. This is the greatest proof of the bondage of the will. Our supposed freedom cannot stop until it has done away with God altogether and only when that happens will we at last see. "You have not chosen me," Jesus said, "I have chosen you." And so it is. We patients cannot be cured on our own terms, but must die to be raised again. His death becomes our death. He dies for us. He dies to get us. This is God's cure worked by Jesus. The cure is death and new life.

God comes to give us a new destiny, a new future, to give us the life of freedom, to give us creation back again. Everything depends on his giving it to us freely, unconditionally, actually, concretely. It is his action, his pronouncement, his actual saying it to us, here in our time and place, that is of the essence. Just as in defining the nature of freedom and bondage where the concern was not with theory but with actuality, so also with God's action; with his election and predestination the concern is not with theory —with what might or might not have happened "up in heaven"— but with actuality. The concern is with what God actually does in and through the deed of Christ and the preaching and sacraments that are authorized by it. The preaching and the sacrament, the actual saying and doing of the "I forgive you," "I love you," *is* the carrying out of God's immutable resolve, on the plane of our history. Nothing can actually save us but that predestination— God's actual saying of the word to us. Every turn we make in attempting to solve the matter on a theoretical level only leads us deeper into bondage, out of the frying pan into the fire. Only the concrete "I love you" can help. We can be saved only by hearing and believing that word. That is death to all that is past and resurrection to the new. God does not call off his almightiness in saving us, he carries it out. He proves himself to be almighty even over me! Once again it must be seen as a matter of death and new life. The Confessional point is lost if one "chickens out" and compromises the so-called polemical exaggerations in the face of all the questions. Perhaps we can construct a little parable to illustrate the matter. Suppose there is a lowly peasant lad who has a secret love for a beautiful princess. It seems a hopeless, lost love. He fears he can't have her so he only worships from afar. In his hurt he takes steps to defend himself. He constructs a kind of defense mechanism, a kind of "fictional theology" about her if you will. He tells himself that she is too vain and proud for her own good. She consorts with all the wrong people—with princes, not with peasant lads. Yet he dreams that maybe he can make it somehow. He sets out to show her. He sets out to become rich and powerful. He plans and plots and sets ideals for himself. He dreams of himself as a potential prince! But then to top it all off he hears that she has already been predestined for someone. She has already decided the matter. That, of course, would be the last, crushing blow. But he refuses to believe it and goes on doggedly pursuing his ideals and perhaps even begins to become cruel and ruthless in his frustration and anger.

Then suppose one fine day the royal carriage comes clattering down the road and pulls up at the door. The princess steps down and comes to him and announces, "John, what in the world are you up to? Don't you see? You are the one I have decided on! I love you and always have. Why are you making such a fool of yourself?"

"Who me? Holy Smokes!"

Now, in theology, of course, at that point we say, Holy Spirit! The word is spoken. The "royal carriage" has arrived. What was hidden is revealed. Only that word, nothing else, can save from all the nonsense, all the self-imposed bondage. No theory, no amount of speculation about the "princess" can do it. One only gets farther into the woods of one's own fictions. Once the word has been spoken he can let it all be. Why should he want to change the predestination or oppose it now? At last it can be seen that all the dreams, the "theology" he had made up was just a fiction, a defense mechanism against the truth. He can believe and love and be saved. He has new life.

The story, of course, is somewhat romantic. To be more accurate theologically in the biblical and Confessional sense we would have to say that when the royal carriage came we were so incensed that all our plans and ideals had been for naught, we rose up and killed the royal lover, put him on a cross. For in our bondage we loved the darkness rather than the light. But the One crucified rose and came back to say, "Shalom, you are mine, I have chosen you nevertheless!"

That is what the divine election and predestination is about. What was hidden is revealed. The only thing that can cure our bondage is the coming, the actual coming of the lover. We worry and fuss about all the theory because, like the peasant lad, we don't know whom the princess has in mind. But the answer is revealed. The answer is always: you. The fact that it is said to you is the proof of it. God, I expect, knows that he is a problem for us. But he has undertaken to solve that problem himself—by his coming to us in Jesus, in preaching, in the sacraments. *You* are the one. That is the point of the Reformation *pro me:* it is for me, for you. The preacher has the unheard of authority to say that, to carry out the divine election. "All authority," Jesus said, "in heaven and on earth has been given unto me . . . , go ye therefore . . . !" (Matt. 28:19).

In the light of this concrete word there is passage from death to life; there is new birth, regeneration. In the light of the concrete word all the old questions and protestations should simply begin to fade away. "We do have a choice, don't we?" Imagine saying that when confronted like Mary Magdalene by the Almighty Lover risen from the tomb! As Augustine knew, insistence on freedom of choice is, in the final analysis, the mark of the disintegration of the will—a will unable to "make up its mind," torn this way and that by conflicting desires. When at least one is "gotten at," when one is claimed, one speaks a different language. One says, "My Lord and my God! The way is plain. I have no choice." God has claimed me. One doesn't preach merely to give people a choice. One preaches until people at last might say, "I have no choice. I am completely taken." For me to live is Christ, and to die is gain! As Col. 3:3 has it, "For you have died, and your life is hid with Christ in God." There is new life from death.

The way of evangelical theology lies ahead, beyond, through all the questions and protestations, not in retreat and compromise. "But we can say no, can't we?" In the light of the concrete word, the arrival of the "royal carriage" at your door, such questions must be answered differently. "What in the world do you want to do that for?" The "royal carriage" arrives, and you greet the lover with a question like that? "But, but, I can say no, can't I?" Perhaps an even better reply would be, "Can you? Speak for yourself!" Take care! The answer will be a confession! Holding out for the ability to say no can be just another mark of the disintegration of the will. It is like building an escape clause into a marriage contract—a practice all too familiar these days. "I can say no, can't I?—when the next one comes along, or the going gets rough? Such language just does fit the nature of the case. Formally, of course, it is not a matter of force. Luther and the Confessions insist on that as well—insofar as the persistent question about being able to say no wants to assert that it has its place. But it is a matter of power—the power of the gospel to break our bondage and save us to say "yea" and "amen," to bring us out of death to life.

The same goes even for much of our traditional fear about the irresistibility of grace. In our penchant for abstract theory we tend to think of it as though it were some sort of force, a mysterious pulling of strings behind the scenes by which we are somehow compelled against our wills to salvation whether we like it or not. No doubt much that has been said about irresistible grace is something like that. But once understood that it is not force but *grace* that we are talking about, that concrete "I love you" of the crucified and risen one, then we should not shy away too quickly. So when the question is put, "You don't mean to say grace is irresistible do you?" I think it more consonant with the truth of the matter to answer, "Yes, I find it to be so, don't you?" Likewise for old questions such as, "Do you mean to say once saved, always saved?" Again, perhaps the best answer would be "What's the matter with that? I would hope so, wouldn't you?" That is what Luther means by saying, "The Holy Spirit is no skeptic and the things he has written in our hearts are not doubts or opinions, but assertions—surer and more certain than sense and life itself."[13]

Once again, the questions betray us. They are a part of the defense mechanism, the death rattle of the Old Adam who is under radical attack and resorts to the last strategy—the attempt to put us on the defensive, to throw all the blame for lack of freedom and responsibility on the gospel. Evangelical and Reformation Confessional theology cannot give in to that strategy. It has done so for too long. It is the gospel that brings freedom possibility, newness, love, and hope. Usually the biggest objection to what we have been trying to say is that the Reformation position does not leave room for human responsibility. If God rules all things and predestines, how is there room for human moral responsibility? No doubt there is a great deal to be said about this issue which would take us somewhat afield. But here what can be said is that true human responsibility begins in the moment we are grasped by the concrete word in such a fashion that we open our lips to confess our sin, our bondage, our blindness and sing God's praises. Responsibility comes when we see ourselves precisely in the light of the justification address as *simul iustus et peccator*. It begins when we see at last that what we might have claimed as responsibility was all sham and fiction, like the "responsibility" of the peasant lad trying to make himself fit for the princess according to his incredibly false estimate of things. It is the very claim to such freedom that is the mark of irresponsibility. True responsibility is part of the gift of grace itself. God does not come to us because we are free and responsible. He comes all the way to us because we are not and he intends to make us so. He comes to set us free and to give us that destiny which he himself has planned for us as his creatures. He comes to set us free from our bondage, our illusions, dreams and fictions, our enslavement to our own ideals, to the law. He comes to give us the freedom to live, to bring forth life out of death. To find *that* freedom is our God-given predestination!

5

THE WORD OF LIFE

We come now to the matter of proclamation and the pesky but persistent question of its relevance. It may be a mistake to leave that question until last. Had I followed at least some versions of the "law-gospel" method I should have spent some time first analyzing the human situation to which the message of justification as here developed is to be applied. Justification could then have been inserted easily into the place made for it and its "relevance" become immediately apparent. There are some considerations, however, which have impelled me to the order I have followed. I hope these will become clear as we proceed. Not the least of these is that it is generally better to get some idea of what it is we are talking about before we attempt to define its relevance. Indeed, if the thing itself is set forth with some clarity, its relevance should be more or less apparent without a lot of argument.

We begin with Article V on the Office of the Ministry:

> To obtain such faith [the justifying faith defined by Article IV] God instituted the office of ministry, that is, provided the Gospel and the sacraments. Through these, as through means, he gives the Holy Spirit, who works faith, when and where he pleases, in those who hear the Gospel. And the Gospel teaches that we have a gracious God, not by our own merits but by the merit of Christ, when we believe this.[1]

The article directs us to the proclamation of the justifying word. If justification is a decree, a pronouncement, then it must be pronounced, preached. Through that the Spirit works faith when and where he pleases and calls the church into being.

We do have a problem with what we call "relevance" today.

It appears to many as though we have this wonderful "cure" but no one seems to have the disease any longer. Or worse, the situation might be similar to that with smallpox vaccine: it is no longer administered because the vaccination causes more harm and kills more people than the disease! In any case, questions persist about the relevance of the proclamation of unconditional justification. It is, of course, important to recall that such questions are not particularly new. Paul had trouble convincing his contemporaries of the relevance of his message to their "needs," as did Augustine and the Reformers and just about anyone who ever got caught in the beam of light that message focuses on our darkness. But for all that, we must—I suppose—take cognizance of the way in which the questions arise in our time. They go something like this. Does not concern for justification depend too much on the experience of the anxious conscience, the experience of sin and guilt? Who is concerned about them any more? Some perhaps, but certainly not everyone. At least, so we are told. Furthermore, does not the con-centration on justification really stem from Luther's own particular anxieties in face of the penitential system of the late middle ages? Why then should justification be made the plumbline by which everything is measured?

Moving beyond the existential- or personal-problem level one might be driven to ask about the propriety of putting justification at the center of dogmatics or giving it such prominence. There is a movement among exegetes, for instance, to demonstrate that justification is hardly so central or dominant a theme in the scrip-tures. There is, it is said, a whole array of additional images, themes, metaphors, and models upon which one can draw to understand our relationship to God and communicate what it means to be saved. So the hegemony of justification and its relevance comes under attack. It might seem that, with the insistence on death-life language articulated here, I have myself joined in the attack. By trying to insist, however, on the complementarity of the language of justification and the language of death and life, I want to dis-associate myself from that attack. For if the death of the old and the resurrection of the new cannot be explicated in this age without the language of justification, we are committed to upholding its relevance as well.

Perhaps we should begin by asking what we mean by "relevance for today." Conscious attempts to be relevant are constantly abortive, if not embarrassing. Arguments about relevance are usually depressingly dull and finally inconclusive. Probing for the "person of today" to whom one is supposed to be relevant seems to be something of a futile exercise. Just when we got around to excising the language about witchcraft from the Catechism, behold, the world goes on a witchcraft binge! As Karl Barth once put it, one seems always to be running after the train that has just left. Perhaps part of the problem is that we mistake relevance for topicality. The *topical* is that which is peculiar to a particular *topos*, a restricted time and place, styles which come and go, the fads which fade in and fade out like the "stars" which created them, the topics of current interest expatiated upon in TV talk shows mostly by people who have no particular qualification to do so. The topical is here today, gone tomorrow. The relevant, however, is that which lifts out of and above the limitations of mere *topos*, "relieves" us of the burdens of our own narrow place and makes contact with the more universal—that which "always" and "everywhere" applies. Strictly speaking, it is therefore redundant to inquire about what is relevant "for today." If something is relevant at all, it should always be so.

So to be more precise the question should be put thus: Is justification by faith alone relevant or was it only of topical interest? Is it always and everywhere applicable or does it answer only to more or less parochial states and needs of the hyman psyche? Since the time of the Enlightenment there has been a more or less subtle attempt to quarantine justification in a temporal, spacial, and dogmatic isolation ward. Justification is supposed to be limited to the needs of a particular time, a particular place, a particular context and minor role in any dogmatic corpus—perhaps a footnote on page 667. The attempt seems to be to convince us that justification is of merely topical interest. And that is done often with a kind of passion which betrays something more than dispassionate and objective observation!

There are three ways one might go about combatting the claim that justification by faith alone is of merely topical interest. One might be through scriptural exegesis and interpretation itself.

Wilhelm Dantine in his helpful book *The Justification of the Un-Godly*[2] argues quite cogently that wherever one looks in scripture, God is the judge before whom we shall have to stand at last, whether we "feel guilty" or not. If that is at all so, then it would seem that the sentence of the judge might be of some *relevance* to us. Personally, I would have to confess that like most moderns I don't spend much time "feeling guilty." Yet now and then I do have visions of that last great scene when the names and the sentences are to be read out from the Book of Life. Coming down through the F's, will it be there—my name? Will I be there "When the roll is called up yonder?" Sometimes when people ask, "What do I do if I don't feel guilty?", I am tempted to answer, "Maybe the first thing to do is to check your pulse!" There is, it seems to me, *something* relevant about that scene which ought to give us pause—is there not?

New Testament exegetes today are also getting over the tendency to relegate justification language to a minor role. Not only would such downplaying be a fatal mistake as far as the New Testament is concerned, but it would effectively block or erase one of the vital links between the Old Testament and the New Testament. For justification language in the New Testament is precisely the link to the righteousness of God so vital to the Old Testament. It can even be suspected, if not conclusively shown, that oddly enough, one of the roots of the polemic against justification language in members of the *Religionsgeschichtliche Schule* like Paul de Legarde was covert anti-Semitism!

The importance of the language of justification to the scriptures thus goes a long way in dispelling facile arguments from the "variety of images" in scripture. The scripture is not simply a cafeteria of religious options from which to pick and choose depending upon how you happen to "feel" on a given day. The scriptural evidence is that justification language is not merely topical. It *is* central and *relevant*, that is, it lifts us out of the merely topical, our transient "feeling," and brings us face to face with the question of what is always, everywhere, and finally true. It confronts us with the fact that there is an ultimate judge before whom the question of justice, righteousness, is decisive.

No doubt, however, the scriptural evidence or claim does not in itself make vital contact with the "person of today" we are constantly worrying about. What is needed, is precisely to demonstrate that such language can and should be "meaningful" to us today. Thus we might have recourse to the two other ways in which the relevance of it all might come home to us. The first of these ways we might call the attempt to establish the need for justification *sola fide* as unconditional, promise, death and life; and the second more of an attempt to drive to proclaim justification in such a way that the proclamation itself does the deed. If one is to continue the love and marriage analogy one might say that the first way would be something like attempting first to persuade the single person that he or she really needs marriage, while the second would be something like trying simply to present the beauty, appeal, and charm of the lover and let that carry the day. The first would be more apologetic—constructing an apology for marriage; whereas the second would be kerygmatic—presenting the "heavenly bridegroom" himself in all his splendor and appeal. Both of these ways might be possible given the perspective developed in the previous chapters, but there are some considerations—as we shall see—which make me incline more and more to the latter.

Before proceeding, however, we need to be clear that what has been said thus far proposes something of a change in focus for the relevance question. Contending as I have been for the complementarity of justification language and death-life language, has the effect of drawing justification talk away from its strictly juridical rootage and the concern for sin and guilt in legal terms alone. If unconditional justification means the death of the sinner and new life, then the sin and guilt of which we are speaking is precisely that incurred by entrapment in the legal scheme and its pretensions. The sin of which we are guilty is precisely the refusal of new life through our own attempts to remain in the saddle at all costs. In that refusal we will consciously or unconsciously marshall all our forces—both moral and immoral. Even our theology will be enlisted in the service of protection. We use the argument that all that legal talk is not relevant any more, but then in the last extremity turn about and use the law and legal talk precisely as protection against the final question over our lives. After all, we do have to do *something*, don't we? Ah yes, . . . just as long as it is not so much as to give us a "guilt trip." (To put a "guilt trip" on someone is, of course, about the worst thing you can do these days!) We will scorn those who use the law for guilt-tripping us, but then in our desperation turn about and use it as protection against the *sola gratia*. So we remain stuck fast and bound—but not to anything great or passionate, just to penny-ante Christianity and a cut-rate gospel. The sin which has to be exposed is not legal as such, but lethal—it is a matter of death and life.

So the relevance question has to be refocused. If one were to use Freudian language perhaps one could say that putting justification language and death-life language together involves a shift in focus from the super-ego to the ego. Justification language understood only in the terms of the legal metaphor is language which focuses on the super-ego, the "conscience" of the moral person within a given, more or less intact system of unquestioned laws and values. Justification "by grace through faith" is comfort to the conscience, the super-ego, while the ego goes more or less unscathed. The I, the subject, still survives. "Faith" is an active verb made possible by "grace" in such a way that the continuity of the "ego" is not seriously disrupted.

It is precisely *this* understanding of justification language which we say is no longer "relevant." The super-ego, the "conscience" of today is no longer vitally engaged or activated by an intact system of unquestioned values. At most we will resort to it only when trying to protect ourselves from attack. Then we will protest loudly against infringements on our "integrity" and "moral responsibility."

Justification *sola fide* understood as death and life, however, shifts the focus to the ego and its very continuity. It becomes a matter of the death of the ego and new life. This is signalled exactly by the kind of questions we raise over against such a proclamation: *I* have to do something, don't I? We are willing, if need be, to admit that our vices should go, but certainly not our virtues. We persist in picturing ourselves as "virtuous" persons—at least to some degree.

Now if this is actually the case, how in the world shall I argue for relevance? I might be able to persuade the super-ego of the error of its ways and get it to "accept" grace because I appeal to its basic moral sensibilities, its *raison d'être,* but how shall I entice the ego to its own death? "Will you come into my parlor, said the spider to the fly? How can that work? Or would it even be honest? Can the ego will its own death? It might, perhaps, in some abstract allegorical or mystical sense. But actually? This, of course, was the nub of the issue between Luther and Erasmus. When Erasmus wanted to insist that the free will (the ego) can "will or not will those things that pertain to salvation," Luther replied:

> Now, since death, the cross, and all the evils of the world are numbered among the works of God that lead to salvation, the human will will thus be able to will its own death and perdition. Yes, it can will all things when it can will the contents of the word and work of God. . . . But what is here left to grace and the Holy Ghost? This plainly to ascribe divinity to "free will!" For to will the law and the gospel, not to will sin, and to will death, is possible to divine power alone, as Paul says in more places than one.[3]

What makes a treatise like *The Bondage of the Will* so upsetting is that it is a mighty attack on the ego and all its pretensions. That is why for the most part we find it possible to live with everything else Luther wrote except *The Bondage of the Will.* But even at that, we have been able to get along with him in all his other writings only as long as we can successfully extricate the super-ego language for our comfort and protection and turn a blind eye to all the language about death and life—the fundamental attack on the ego and its identity. And I expect we do the same with the scriptures! What makes *The Bondage of the Will* so difficult is that it affords us practically no possibility for so doing. Luther considered the issue joined there to be the *cardo rerum;* he always believed that *The Bondage of the Will,* along with the Catechisms, was his major testament to posterity. Perhaps, in the light of our analysis, we might begin to get some glimpse of why he thought this. In *The Bondage of The Will* all the extraneous super-ego issues are stripped away and we are left with the question of the ego facing the matter of death and life. "Faith alone" is not a remedy for the super-ego in the attempts to gain virtue. It is an attack on the ego which will make or break us.

In such a situation, how shall one argue for relevance? Can we persuade the ego of its "need" to die? That would be like what we referred to earlier as attempting to persuade the happy single person of the need to get married—a difficult task. The theology of death and life is simply not relevant to the Old Adam or Eve directly precisely because it spells death to such old being. Perhaps one of our greatest miscalculations since the Reformation was to assume that the gospel is relevant to us as we are and to think we could somehow make it relevant to our "needs" in some direct or positive fashion.

If we are going to argue in this vein for relevance today the case would have to be made indirectly and negatively. The argument would have to be quite ruthless and unrelenting. The best example of such argument is perhaps Ernest Becker's *Denial of Death*.[4] That study is an unrelenting exposé of the ego's attempt to protect itself from death and consequently from life—an interesting corroboration of much we have been developing here. If one is looking for a "point of contact" there could hardly be one more universal than the fact that we are all going to die—and we can't take it. Unlike other animals we know we are going to die and we cannot bear it. We cannot bear our finitude. Our whole life's project is to deny death. It is incredible to us that we should be nothing more than complicated food for worms. We are under the serpent's seductive whisper: "You shall not die, you shall be as gods." We must embark on "our own cause" (*causa sui*). The very tenor and structure of the life we lead is poisoned by our fear and denial of death. It is death—and the way we deal with it—that controls our life. This is exactly the situation outlined by Luther in *The Bondage of the Will*. We must, we are bound to, build our own defenses against death. We "need" protection against death; hence we construct the lie—the vital lie—of character morality and maturity. But the very thing we need to live, to protect ourselves from all the terror and beauty of creation, becomes our prison. We are trapped in our own lie. In order to sum up the matter "once and for all, for all future psychoanalysis and students of man," Becker quotes from Otto Rank: "Every human being is . . . equally unfree, that is, we . . . create out of freedom a prison. . . . "[5] Poor old Howard Hughes life was in this respect almost a perfect modern rendition of the "Parable of the Rich Fool" and indicative of the fate of all of us. He was so afraid of death that lo and behold in the end it killed him! He lived by making his fortune on instruments of death. Afraid of pollution and contamination he walled himself up in seclusion. He was so successful in denying death that it killed him. When the time came, no one could get to him. And what of us? Can anyone get to us before its too late? Jesus, we are told, partook of our nature, "that through death, he might destroy him who has the power of death, that is the devil, and deliver all those who through fear of death were subject to lifelong bondage." (Heb. 2:14–15). That fits exactly! It is, after all, the New Testament message.

Thus there is the possibility of arguing in an indirect and negative way for the relevance of the message. The argument takes the form of an attack on the ego and its desperate follies, its sickness unto death. But will it work as a sustained method? There are several considerations which give me, personally, pause. First of all, will people really believe someone like Becker? How could he be any more successful than any other—this voice crying into the wilderness? We know all the protests. He is much too gloomy and pessimistic. Life isn't really *that* bad, is it? Isn't he some kind of strange dualist? His view is caught in the trap of individualism. The world will build defenses of this sort against such an argument and go its relentless way. Who reads Becker anymore? The book is given the Pulitzer prize, to be sure, but maybe that is only the world's kiss of death. It will soon be out of print and we will go on to Erma Bombeck and a million other things. The problem at the deepest level is that the old being, the old age, is simply not able to take an analysis so ruthless and unrelenting as that of Becker unless there is *some* hope somewhere, some light at the end of the tunnel. If there is no new life, no resurrection, then denial of death is our only protection. Our vital lies and illusions are better than death. If there is no promised land we are better off going back to Egypt. The kind of analysis Becker offers—true as it might be—cannot and will not be taken unless it can be seen in the light of Easter morning. But if that is so, how can we *start* with it?

In the second place, there is a sense in which even to take this kind of indirect approach to the question of death and life and attempt to render it dogmatically into a *method* in some self-conscious way is to run the risk of deceiving and dissembling. The temptation lies near at hand to mistake the distinctions between super-ego and ego for existential reality and thus to think the matter "solved," so we can just "apply" what we have been talking about to "them." When we make the distinction between super-ego, and ego, for instance, we will then say, perhaps, "Aha! Yes! Now I understand what you are talking about." "Now I see where you are coming from!" And one will then think that it is all clear, so that the very threat, the attack on the ego is as a matter of fact comprehended and thus obviated. Once we "understand" it, all we need do is apply it! Once we understand, once what is said in *The Bondage of the Will* is conceptually clarified, the "problem" is solved. Once I know the trap and the poison, I can play the spider to the fly.

I really have serious reservations about that sort of procedure. We need to be aware of the ways in which even our theologizing is part of the protective game—the extent to which it too participates in the "vital lie." The distinctions, the apparatus we use, are helpful as an analytical tool, but in the end they too must get out of the way, if possible, for the thing itself.

This brings me to a third question about proceeding in that fashion. The question is, can we, can I, handle it? My answer to this question will have to take on, theologically speaking, something of the aspect of an *Apologia Pro Vita Mea* which will explain if not excuse the method reflected in these chapters and provide a kind of prelude to what I want to say in conclusion about preaching. I was convinced for one reason or another early on in my theological career that I had to go the way of the theology of the cross as indicated by Luther, and that led inexorably in the direction of *The Bondage of the Will* and the law-gospel dialectic. It was and is the only kind of theology I can believe and work with. Much more could be said about that but this is not the place to do it. The point I want to make here is that when I came to the task of preaching and tried to begin by exposing the need for the message as it supposedly developed out of analysis of the human situation or the experience of the law, I was always uneasy; I was never quite confident that I could make it work properly so as to arrive at the goal toward which I was striving, namely, a genuine "Word of Life," genuine "Good News." Sometimes it seemed to work and of course people were gracious about it all, but most of the time I wasn't really satisfied. I couldn't get away from the suspicion that I was manipulating people. They might be gratified in a masochistic way by having been given their weekly flogging but what's the use of that?

I found myself struggling with the problem of preaching on the basis of a *theologia crucis*. To make a long story short, I gradually came to realize that my efforts to develop first the "need" for the gospel—my struggle with the problem of "relevance"—did not consistently accomplish what I was aiming at. To use the language of death and life, it occurred to me that I was *not* putting the Old Adam or Eve to death very successfully but, precisely by concentrating so much on their problems, only prolonging the agony. I wasn't putting them out of their misery with the *coup de grâce;* I was only helping them grovel around in it. That is, I was letting the Old Adam and Eve set the agenda. The result was that I would often dig holes so deep I could hardly get out, and could in the end offer little else than a bit of dime-store psychological comfort. I began to fear that all I was doing was manipulating the Old Adam psychologically. To this day I have a very hard time listening to sermons of that sort. When the pastor begins by "exposing" the "human situation" in some way or other I have a tendency to slide down in the pew and say to myself, "Come on, Reverend, I know things are bad. I read the newspaper and *Time* magazine and even a little psychology. When are you going to get to the point and give it to me "straight up" from the text?"

So I have begun to wonder if the "relevance" approach does not have some flaws—especially if followed exclusively. If the message is indeed an attack on the ego, if it is a matter of death and new life, a different strategy is probably called for. Ethical and social concerns raise the question as well. Concentrating on

91

the super-ego or trying to develop an apology only on the basis of "need" ends finally by succumbing to the old charge of individualism. Social activists in our time have tried to counter the impasse by appealing to communal and collective concerns for justice. What moderns need, we are told, is not a gracious God, but a gracious neighbor. So, shunting aside the problem of the ego and its death we set out somewhat reluctantly and grudgingly to be a "gracious neighbor." But it hasn't worked. The wheel would not turn and we seem to be running out of gas and turning back to old individualistic enticements, cultivating a private spirituality. We must think more about how the death of the old ego and the rebirth of the new *overcomes* our individualism and makes us members of the body of the risen Lord.

In the light of these considerations I have come to think that we might have more success if we could just present the bride in all her beauty (or in this case the heavenly bridegroom!) rather than exhausting all our energy constructing an apology for marriage. Would we not get farther if we could just say, "Here he is and he is for you all the way, no strings attached?" No doubt there would be risks in attempting to do that. The major risk is that the Old Being in us will attempt simply to take advantage of it. It could be presented as sheer romantic slop or cheap psychological comfort that solidifies protection against the death of the old and the resurrection of the new—which is what happens in much modern "sweet Jesus" piety.

Theologically one might fall prey to the Barthian error of thinking one can preach gospel before law. If the matter is truly one of death and life as we have been insisting, it should be obvious that this cannot be done. Formally, one can indeed speak gospel words first, or at least try to. The problem does not lie there. The problem lies in the fact that the Old Being will not and cannot *hear* gospel no matter what one says. The Old Being will only use whatever is said as part of the protection, solidification in the *causa sui* project, and translate it into or see it as a ratification of the legal system. That is, the Old Being will turn *whatever one says* into law. It is impossible, therefore, to set out to preach gospel first, as if there were some sort of methodological key to the matter.

It would seem as though, methodologically, we are effectively stymied. If one begins with the law in the sense of trying to establish need or grovel about in "gloom, despair, and agony" one rarely gets out of the hole and usually ends up just prolonging the agony of the Old Adam or by capitulating. If one tries to shift to gospel first, that will only be misused by the Old Being to solidify its defenses. What is one to do? It is precisely here that the approach used in these chapters—which is basic to the Lutheran tradition itself—is helpful. If justification by faith alone is death and resurrection, then it is the proclamation of that justification itself that does the deed we are looking for. It is the proclamation itself that puts to death and raises up—at one and the same time. But if that is the case, then one would not look to the exposé of the human predicament to do the work of the law, or even necessarily to provide the "point of contact" for the relevance of it all. One would not be busily digging holes one can never get out of. One would depend rather upon the unconditional word itself to do the job. It is the very unconditionality, the "nothing to be done," itself that administers the *coup de grâce*, because it kills and makes alive at once. The preacher, that is, leads from strength, announcing the unconditional word, knowing that in the first instance it is not going to be heard as gospel by the Old Being because it is an attack on the ego, the beginning of the end, so that the new can start.

When we think about preaching, about "delivering the goods" and the place of justification language today, the CA can be helpful: "To obtain such faith (justifying faith) God instituted the office of the ministry, that is, provided the Gospel and the sacraments. Through these as through means, he gives the Holy Spirit, who works faith, when and where he pleases, in those who hear the Gospel." It is clear from this that if justification is a pronouncement, then it has to be pronounced from without. Ministry is the office of speaking this pronouncement, this external word, speaking the unconditional promise; it is the office instituted by God through which God intends to speak, just as the sacraments are means through which God does the acting—and all of this without our own preparations, thoughts and works. Preaching is basically a "doing" of the text to the hearers. Preaching is doing once again in the present what the text authorizes us to do. The text itself is usually an account of what God did, what Jesus did, what the Apostles did in Jesus' name, and of what that did to the hearers. Often we are told just how the hearers reacted. They were astonished, amazed, offended, shocked, angered, comforted, blessed, or they praised God. If that is what the text once did, perhaps we ought to undertake to do it again!

Methodologically, this suggests that perhaps we should, in general, lead from the text, not from the human situation as such. It is the text that is going to do the slaying and the making alive, not any of our grovelling about in the human situation. Thus more and more I find myself looking for just that sort of thing in a text— the word which is a kind of startling abbreviation of the gospel— stark, unconditional. Often, I notice, that very word is a "hard saying," the pronouncement that shocked, the announcement of mercy and forgiveness, the action that amazed and astonished, or even caused the hearers to take up stones to kill! I look for that and often lead with it, knowing full well that it is not at first going to help, that it is likely to be received not as relevant but as a frontal attack on the "ego" of the Old Adam. That too is why, when I talk about the Confessions as I have done here, I tend to lead with the *sola fide*, the "nothing," the unconditional word that is both attack and promise. I believe it is that word which is ultimately "relevant"—which will finally bring "relief," lift us out of our self-made prisons—precisely because it *is* a frontal attack on all our defenses. Then, after letting the text set the agenda, I can go on and develop the material—calling on as much analysis of the current human scene and predicament as seems useful and helpful, always, however, with the goal of returning again finally to the pronouncement, the hard saying, the announcement, so that it will finally be heard as the word of life, the gospel, the unconditional word. In other words, whereas first it will be heard as an attack on the "ego", a word which brings death, the aim is that in the end it will be reheard as a word of life.

But that means that in the end we return to the word of justification, the word of the forgiveness of sins, flat out, unconditional, as the last word, the last judgment. I find it hard to escape from just those words, that kind of pronouncement. The reason is basically that only those kinds of words lend themselves to the pronouncement we *can* make in speaking finally for God: I declare you just for Jesus' sake; I declare unto you the forgiveness of all your sins. When it comes down at last to actually saying, pronouncing what we are authorized to say for God from first to second persons, me to you, we don't have many choices. The scriptures, to be sure, have many images for the restoration of our relationship to God, many images for the divine revelation to us. There is reconciliation, rebirth, victory, ransom, redemption, love, truth, light. The problem, however, is that most of those tend to remain just what they are—images, *descriptions* of the relationship or the revelation; but they don't actually do it, make it, directly. They may be enlightening, edifying, even inspiring and so forth, but they don't *do the deed.* To use an analogy, there are many helpful and inspiring, enticing, even normative ways to *describe* the love and marriage relationship, but only the direct, "I love you" or the "I pronounce you husband and wife" *does it.*

When the Reformers and the Confessions latched onto the language of justification and the forgiveness of sins it was not merely that they were hung up on the legal terminology or the experience of guilt as such. What they sought was a language that does the speaking of the gospel directly and does not merely give descriptions of it. They sought a particular kind of speaking which they called gospel speaking as distinguished from all other kinds of speaking which tend to be law. Gospel speaking, unconditional, concrete, first to second person, I to you speaking, furthermore, has to be *present tense* speaking. It cannot be merely a report about what God has done in the past. It is certainly based on that and flows from that but, finally, it has to issue in present tense proclamation. It is like "I baptize you . . ." *here and now,* "I declare unto you the forgiveness of all your sins . . . " "This is my body, given for you . . ." "I declare you just for Jesus' sake." It has to be a speaking which *does* the deed *hinc et nunc.*

But how many statements of that sort can I make? Just what is my "office?" Eric Gritsch and Robert Jenson speak of justification by faith as a metalinguistic proposal of dogma to the church catholic.[6] By that is meant that justification by faith alone does not limit us to one particular content but is rather a stipulation about what constitutes gospel speaking, whatever the content.

gospel speaking is the unconditional, present-tense declaration authorized by the one who died and rose. Yet I find myself wondering how many possibilities there are for my speaking such language, how many options I have. The most immediate and obvious candidate for such language is a statement like, "I declare to you the forgiveness of all your sins for Jesus' sake." That is language which *does* the deed, it does not just talk *about* it. I suspect that this is what the Reformers were after and this is why such language gained such prominence. "I forgive you," "I baptize you," "I give you the body and blood," and perhaps, "I declare you just for Jesus' sake"—that kind of thing I can say and do in carrying out the office entrusted.

The point is that in the final analysis images, paradigms, and models won't do in exercising the office. They talk *about* the relationship but they don't *make* it. No doubt the proclamation will include a great deal of such talk *about* the relationship and that will be necessary, illuminating, and inspiring talk if the preacher is clever and it is done well. But in the final analysis one has to *make* it. One has to *deliver* the goods. One has to come out of the woods, move into the present tense, and exercise the *office* authorized. Here, I say, the possibilities seem to be reduced drastically. One cannot merely play around, publicly, with images. There are a lot of things that don't really help, things which in the final exercise of the office I cannot really say. I can't say, for instance, "I love you," in speaking for God. The "I" gets in the way and confuses the issue. I can only *report* on the fact that *God* loves you, or that "God so loved the world that he gave his Son," but then I have slipped out of that first to second person, I to you, discourse into the third person and even into the past tense—God *loved* the world—and then the *office* goes begging. You don't need me to tell you that. You can read all that in the Bible or even in Paul Tillich! The question is what can *I* say here and now?

Some like to say, for instance, that the theme of "reconciliation" is more prominent than forgiveness or justification language. But what can I do with that? I can, of course, report that "God *was* in Christ reconciling the world unto himself," and that is certainly true and the root of everything. But it is third person talk, past tense. The best I can do on the basis of such talk is then turn and make an appeal, as Paul did, "Be reconciled." But that only tends to throw the ball back in your court, and I shirk my office if I say nothing more.

My point is that in the exercise of the office—the "I say to you" unconditional, present tense pronouncement—we have to return to the language of forgiveness, the language of justification, the "I baptize you." That sort of language we can speak; we are authorized to do so. I expect that is why at last we keep on saying it liturgically and even kerygmatically, though theologically we tell ourselves it is no longer "relevant." In the exercise of the office we don't have much more to say. At the very least, we have to look on these words as paradigmatic for what we must say, whatever the content. We cannot be content merely to *report about* God or the text, we must *do* it, do what the text authorizes us to do in the present, exercise the office. That is the word of life. This is what it means to say that the doctrine of justification is the article by which the church stands or falls. It isn't the doctrine as such that matters, it is this way of speaking, this exercise of the office. When we forget or forbid or put the damper on this way of speaking the church has lost its reason for being.

I must let the word, the text, *do* it. To accomplish that I must attempt to do the text again in the present to its present hearers. I have to get out of the way of the text, the word, so it can have its way with us. For me, a large part of the task of systematic theology is just that—the art of getting out of the way of the text, getting out of the way for Jesus. Much of what I have said in these chapters may have been poorly put, or the strategy mistaken. But I have had one aim in mind—to establish the point that in the end we have to *say* it, pronounce it, do it again. The aim is to unlock, unleash once again the power of the gospel, the power of that word which does indeed judge, confront, attack, kill the old in order to give birth to the new. The art of doing that has perhaps been lost in a sea of images, options, myths, and paradigms. My hope is that we might at least think about how to regain the art of speaking the unconditional word and promise with power.

NOTES

CHAPTER 1

1. See, for instance, Vinzenz Pfnür, "Recognition of the Augsburg Confession by the Catholic Church?" in: *The Role of the Augsburg Confession: Catholic and Lutheran Views,* ed. Joseph A. Burgess (Philadelphia: Fortress Press, 1980), p. 8 and H. Schuette, ibid., pp. 51ff.

2. H. Bornkamm, "Augsburger Bekenntnis," *RGG* 1:175.

3. See *Currents in Theology and Mission* 7 (April 1980): 72ff., where major attitudes of Lutherans in this country are outlined.

4. Vinzenz Pfnür, *Einig in der Rechtfertigunslehre?* (Wiesbaden: Franz Steiner Verlag GMBH, 1970).

5. Joseph Kardinal Ratzinger, "Anmerkungen zur Frage einer 'Anerkennung' der Confessio Augustana durch die katholische Kirche," *Muenchener Theologische Zeitschrift* (29 Jahrgang, Helt 3, 1978): 225ff.

6. Peter Manns, "Zum Vorhaben einer katholischen Anerkennung der Confessio Augustana: Oekumene auf Kosten Martin Luthers?" *Oekumenische Rundschau* 27 (1977): 426–450.

7. Even some Roman Catholics sense this. Joseph Lortz, for instance, sees already in the CA of "Melanchthon the Humanist" the inroads of a trivializing of dogma and relativizing of what is Christian in the Lutheran movement. Melanchthon "ironed out" the roughness and internal contradictions of Luther's thought and in the process . . . "the indestructible quality, the infinite growing potential, that which cannot be taught in the classroom, in short, the primeval quality had been destroyed also." Joseph Lortz, *The Reformation in Germany,* trans. R. Walls (New York: Herder and Herder, 1968), V. 2, p. 61. Pfnür, on the other hand, finds such assertions "monstrous." Pfnür, "Recognition," p. 6.

8. Ratzinger, "Anmerkungen," p. 229.

9. The work of Gerhard Ebeling is perhaps the best introduction to

this development. See, for instance, his *Luther: An Introduction* (Philadelphia: Fortress Press, 1970).

10. Luther's different hermeneutic leads to a different authority structure and thus a different ecclesiology. Where one tries to move from the "dead" letter to the "life-giving spirit" in allegorical fashion, one needs assurance as to which "interpretation" is "right." An authoritative office is demanded by the hermeneutic itself. Where the word actually kills and makes alive matters are quite different. The one so killed and made alive needs no earthly structure to *guarantee* the "doctrine." Where death and resurrection are not reckoned with theologically, however, such "asurrance" can only be misunderstood as "psychological" egotism and "subjectivism." The system which does not entertain the fact of death and life through the word operates only with a kind of antithesis between the ontological and the psychological. Hence Roman Catholics seem able to understand Lutheranism only as a kind of "psychologism" or "existentialism" whose main point is to translate abstract ontological language into the language of "personal experience" and "assurance of salvation" on a subjective level—the consolation of the "terrified conscience." When the theological significance of death-life language is not grasped one tends only to pit ontology against psychology in the continuum of "deathless" being.

11. LW 39, p. 183.

12. LW 26, pp. 67–68 (italics added).

13. Ibid., p. 68.

14. Martin Luther, *The Bondage of the Will*, trans. J. I. Packer and O. R. Johnston (Westwood: Fleming H. Revel Co., 1957), p. 101.

15. Ernest Becker, *The Denial of Death* (New York: Free Press, 1973).

16. Albert Schweitzer, *The Mysticism of Paul the Apostle*, trans. William Montgomery (New York: Henry Holt and Co., 1931), pp. 223ff.

CHAPTER 2

1. *Book of Concord: The Confessions of the Evangelical Lutheran Church*, ed. Theodore G. Tappert (Philadelphia: Fortress Press, 1959), p. 30.

2. Eric W. Gritsch and Robert W. Jenson, *Lutheranism: The Theological Movement and its Confessional Writings* (Philadelphia: Fortress Press, 1976), pp. 7ff, 42ff.

3. Thomas Aquinas, "Summa Theologica," I II ac, Q.113, Art. 6, in *Nature and Grace*, ed. A. M. Fairweather, Library of Christian Classics 11 (Philadelphia: Westminster Press), pp. 192–193.

4. Martin Luther, *Lectures on Romans*, ed. W. Pauck, Library of Christian Classics 15 (Philadelphia: Westminster Press), p. 128.

5. Ibid, pp. 127ff. See also Leif Grane, *Modus Loquendi Theologicus: Luthers Kampf um die Erneurung der Theologie (1515–1518)*, trans. E. Groetzinger (Leiden: E. J. Brill, 1975), pp. 75ff.

6. WA 40, I, p. 280, 3ff. LW 26: p. 165.

7. Ibid.

8. Luther, *Romans*, pp. 179–80.

CHAPTER 3

1. Albert Schweitzer, *The Mysticism of Paul the Apostle*, trans. William Montgomery, (New York: Henry Holt and Company, 1931), p. 295.

2. Tappert, *Book of Concord*, pp. 31–32.

3. Ibid., pp. 41, 45, 46.

4. WA, 7: p. 142.

5. Vinzenz Pfnür, *Einig in der Rechtfertingunslehre?* (Weisbaden: Franz Steiner Verlag GMBH, 1970), p. 239.

6. WA Br 2; p. 372. LW 48: p. 282.

7. Martin Luther, *The Bondage of the Will*, trans. J. I. Packer and O. R. Johnston (Westwood: Fleming H. Revel Co., 1957), p. 99.

8. Karl Rahner, "Justified and Sinner at the Same Time," *Theological Investigations*, vol. 6 (Baltimore: Helicon Press, 1969), p. 222.

9. Pfnür, *Einig*, p. 259.

10. Vinzenz Pfnür, "Recognition of the Augsburg Confession by the Catholic Church?" in *The Role of the Augsburg Confession*, ed. Joseph A. Burgess (Philadelphia: Fortress Press, 1980), p. 14.

11. Pfnür, *Einig*, p. 260.

12. To brand those who *resisted* the "third use of the law" as "antinomian" is a mistake. Rejecting the third use of the law for the sake of the full eschatological reality of the new life out of death is not antinomian. Such rejection is made precisely to *establish* the law in its full, undiminished right in this age *before* death. Those, however, who disregard the eschatological reality of death and new life have to make peace with law by toning it down and domesticating it. This is *covert* antinomianism.

13. WA 56, 486, 7ff. LW 25: p. 478.

14. Martin Luther, *Lectures on Romans*, ed. W. Pauck, Library of Christian Classics 15 (Philadelphia: Westminster Press, 1961), p. 194.

15. Ibid., p. 14 (italics added).

16. Tappert, *Book of Concord*, p. 349.

17. Ibid., p. 445.

18. LW 26: p. 68.

19. Tappert, *Book of Concord*, p. 45.

20. Ibid., p. 19.
21. LW 35: pp. 370–71.

CHAPTER 4

1. New York: Alfred A. Knopf, 1971.
2. Immanuel Kant, *Religion Within the Limits of Reason Alone,* trans. T. M. Greene and H. H. Hudson (New York: Harper Torch book, 1960), p. 111.
3. Tappert, *Book of Concord,* p. 39.
4. *Ibid.,* pp. 39–40.
5. Martin Luther, *The Bondage of the Will,* trans. J. I. Packer and O. R. Johnston (Westwood: Fleming H. Revell Co., 1957), p. 107.
6. See, for instance, LW 30: p. 40 (Heidelberg Disputation); Luther, *Bondage of the Will,* pp. 79ff.
7. Our churches teach that although God creates and preserves nature, the cause of sin is the will of the wicked, that is, of the devil and ungodly men. If not aided by God, the will of the wicked turns away from God, as Christ says in John 8:44, "When the devil lies, he speaks according to his own nature." Tappert, *Book of Concord,* pp. 40–41.
The translation of the German version: It is taught among us that although almighty God has created and still preserves nature, yet sin is caused in all wicked men and despisers of God by the perverted will. This is the will of the devil and of all ungodly men; as soon as God withdraws his support, the will turns away from God to evil. It is as Christ says in John 8:44, "When the devil lies, he speaks according to his own nature" (pp. 40–41).
8. See Klaus Schwarzwäller, "Vom Lehren der Prädestination zur Lehre von der Prädestination," in Wenzel Lohff and Lewis W. Spitz, eds., *Widerspruch, Dialog und Einigung,* (Stuttgart: Calwer Verlag, 1977), pp. 249–273. Also Joseph Lortz sees the CA as a down-playing of the denial of free will. Cf. *The Role of the Augsburg Confession,* ed. Joseph Burgess (Philadelphia: Fotress Press, 1980), p. 6.
9. Eric W. Gritsch and Robert W. Jenson, *Lutheranism: The Theological Movement and its Confessional Writings* (Philadelphia: Fortress Press, 1976), p. 157.
10. "No even remotely Christian discourse can avoid predestinarian statements. If we are to talk to God in any real way, we thereby talk about some sort of 'predestination'. For the word 'God' is only our label to mark the point, in whatever faith or theology we live by, where the buck stops: God is by platitudinous definition absolute." Ibid., p. 158.
11. Ibid., p. 160.
12. Luther, *Bondage of the Will,* p. 162.
13. Ibid., p. 70.

CHAPTER 5

1. Tappert, *Book of Concord*, p. 31.

2. Trans. Eric W. Gritsch and Ruth Gritsch (St. Louis: Concordia Publishing House, 1968).

3. Luther, *The Bondage of the Will*, trans. J. I. Packer and O. R. Johnston (Westwood: Fleming H. Revel Co., 1957), p. 140.

4. Ibid., passim.

5. Ernest Becker, *The Denial of Death* (New York: Free Press, 1973), p. 62.

6. Eric W. Gritsch & Robert W. Jenson, *Lutheranism: The Theological Movement and its Confessional Writings* (Philadelphia: Fortress Press, 1976), pp. 42–43.